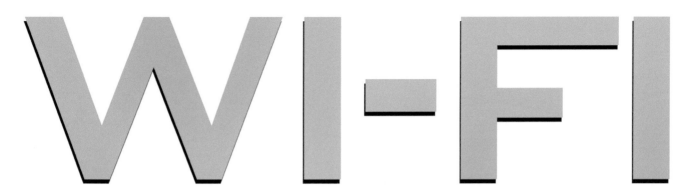

WI-FI
TRACKING IN
RETAIL INDUSTRY

AMITESH SINHA

Copyright © 2015 by Amitesh Sinha. 712155
Library of Congress Control Number: 2015913938

ISBN: Softcover   978-1-5035-9054-0
        Hardcover   978-1-5035-9055-7
        EBook   978-1-5035-9053-3

Rev. date: 09/09/2015

To order additional copies of this book, contact:
Xlibris
1-888-795-4274
www.Xlibris.com
Orders@Xlibris.com

CONTENTS

Disclaimer 1

Synopsis 5

Chapter 1: Introduction to Retailing 7

    What about the Jobs? 8

    Types of Retailers 8

        Store Retailing 8

        Brick-and-Mortar Stores 9

        Specialty Retailing 9

        Nonstore Retailing 10

        The Internet 10

    The Image of Retailers 10

        Social Responsibility 11

    Windows of Opportunity for Retailers 11

    The Rise of Online Businesses and Their Impact on Brick-and-Mortar Stores 12

        As Online and Mobile Shopping Grow 12

        What Does This Mean for Brick-and-Mortar Retailers? 13

Chapter 2: Getting to Know the New Consumer 15

    Twenty-First-Century Retailing 16

    Getting to Know the Modern Consumers 16

        The Consumers Are Instrumented 16

        The Consumers Are More Interconnected 17

        Modern Consumers Are Much More Intelligent 18

    How to Adapt to the Modern Consumer 18

    The Shopping Process 19

        Transformation of the Purchase Cycle 19

Chapter 3: The Rise of E-Commerce 21

    The Requirement for Retail Space 21

    The Positive Side 23

    Size of E-Commerce 23

Chapter 4: Importance of Analytics for Retail 25

    The Opportunities and Challenges 26

    Retail Analytics—A Game Changer 26

        The Importance of Customer Loyalty 26

        Analytics in Customer Loyalty 27

    The Span of Analytical Options 28

        Understanding the Prerequisites of Retail Analytics 29

    Commonly Adopted Analytical Trends in the Retail Industry 29

        Shelf Space Allocation and Assortment Optimization 30

        Customer-Driven Marketing 30

        Fraud Detection and Prevention 30

Integrated Forecasting 30

Clustering and Localization 31

Marketing Mix Modelling 31

Pricing Optimization 31

Chapter 5: Understanding Wi-Fi Tracking **33**

How Wi-Fi Tracking Works 34

Privacy Matters 34

The iConnect Shopper Intelligence Analytics: An Overview 35

How iConnect SIA Works 35

Statistical Sampling 35

Consumers and the Use of Mobile Devices 36

Shopping Trends and Retailers 37

SIA: Use of Wi-Fi Signals 37

Classification of Data 38

SIA and Privacy 40

Chapter 6: When Big Data Meets Business Analytics **43**

Harnessing the Data: Volume, Variety, Veracity, and Velocity 44

Recognizing the Pain Points of Retail 44

Asking the Crucial Questions 45

Extracting Meaning from the Gigantic Amounts of Data 45

An Interconnected Firm 45

The Pillars of Business Analytics 46

Business Intelligence (BI) 46

Advanced Analytics (AA) 46

Performance Management (PM) 47

Analytical Decision Management: The Advantage 47

Making Risk-Aware and Informed Decisions 48

Setting Direction through Strategic Decisions 48

Getting the Visibility to Make Tactical Decisions 49

Making Operational Decisions by Leveraging Real-Time Information 49

Aligning the Outcomes to the Business Strategy 49

The Value of Analytics 50

Aligning around the Impact Point 50

Chapter 7: Marketing in the Customer-Driven Era **53**

Getting to Know the Consumer Behaviour and Trends 54

Utilizing **Customer** Data 54

Putting Data in **Context** **54**

Connecting with the Consumer **Communities** **55**

Keeping the **Content** in Mind 55

Getting to the Personalised **Commerce** Part 55

Analysing Unstructured Data 55

The Challenge of Unstructured Data 56

Identifying the Opportunities Presented by Untapped Analytics 56

Decision-Making Driven by Customers 56

Content Analytics 57

Understanding the Affinities between Customers and Products 57

Advanced Affinity Analysis 57

Market Basket Analysis 58

Understanding Customer Preferences 58

Anticipating the Consumers' Next Move 58

Improving Your Retail Promotions 58

Chapter 8: Making Smart Business Decisions **59**

Enabling Your Merchandising Efficiencies 60

Reuniting Bottom-Up and Top-Down Plans 61

Creating Dynamic Retail Assortments 61

Bringing into Line the Store-Level Assortment with the Demand 61

Developing Supply Chain Driven by Demand 62

Making Use of Proven Technology 63

Empowering Customers to Self-Service Whenever in the Store 63

Increasing Customer Loyalty and Retention 64

Line Busting and Mobile Point-of-Sale 64

Displaying Advertising and Digital Signage 64

Providing Support for a Number of Wi-Fi-Enabled Devices In-Store 65

Getting to Grips with Supply Chain Challenges 65

Getting Visibility across the Supply Chain 66

Solving Operational Problems before They Occur 66

Collaborating with the Vendors 66

Managing Brand Loyalty 67

Building Brand Loyalty in the Digital Era 67

The Challenges of Building Brand Loyalty 68

Putting the Data to Use 69

Meeting the Needs of Today's Consumers 69

The Growth of Mobile Commerce 69

Getting Higher ROI on Marketing Investments 70

Developing Trust with Customers 70

Managing Performance of a Store 70

Incorporating Stores into a Retail Firm's Planning Process 71

Recognizing Ineffective Processes 71

Recognizing Ineffective Technologies 71

Finding a Blueprint for Success 72

Chapter 9: Understanding Social Media in Retail **73**

How It All Begins 74

Customer Involvement 75

'Likes' Do Not Equate to Sales 75

Complaints Gone Viral 76

Maximizing Shopping Experience Using Social Media 76

Chapter 10: Effective Store Performance Management...**79**

Store Operations: The Common Challenges...79

    Shrink...80

    Out of Stock...80

The Fundamental Elements for Successful Daily Store Management...80

    Roles and Responsibilities...81

    Daily Management Routines...81

    Key Performance Indicators and Reporting Structure...82

    Effective Meetings...82

Chapter 11: Understanding the Brick-and-Mortar–Online Retailer Gap...**83**

The Shopping Process...85

    Transformation of the Purchase Cycle...85

How Consumers Interact with the Digital World...86

    Reversing the Effects of Showrooming...86

    How Brick-and-Mortar Stores Are the Future of Retail...86

The Issue of Showrooming...87

Bridging the Gap between Online and Offline Stores...88

One Brand, Same Enhanced Experience, Multiple Channels...88

From Multichannel to Cross-Channel: A Shift in the Approach...89

    Going Cross-Channel...89

Chapter 12: Leveraging IT Solutions...**91**

Building the Foundation for Business Analytics...92

    Moving Rapidly on Actionable Insights...92

How Retailers Can Take Advantage of Emerging Technology...93

Measure...93

Connect...93

Influence...94

IT and Business: Delivering Constant Improvements...94

Conclusion...**95**

About Amitesh Sinha...**97**

Index...**99**

DISCLAIMER

FOREWORD

To be able to successfully manage various aspects of a retail business in today's fast-paced economy, organizations need to be able to effectively meet the needs of the consumers while ensuring that they accomplish other goals, such as the need to operate efficiently and effectively.

Retail analytics provides retailers the ability to make informed decisions that can enhance the performance of their stores and thereby ensure their businesses' success. For retailers to achieve this, they need to be able to utilise crucial data that can help them unlock their true sales potential. However, collection of data has been much more difficult for brick-and-mortar stores compared to that for online retailers, with the latter having a greater control over customer analytics.

A better understanding of how customers behave is crucial to implementing appropriate solutions to enhance their experience and, ultimately, sales for the retailer. With the advent of online retailers, brick-and-mortar stores have come under fire due to the latter's inability to understand the needs of customers in more detail.

E-commerce websites, for instance, can gather analytical data comprising information such as what products the customer has searched for, which products they have browsed for on the website, and much more—all this information can help the e-commerce platform to generate relevant data to personalise the customer's experience.

Online retailers have captured a major portion of the market share; with statistics showing that as many as 69 per cent of Americans frequently buy products online, the numbers are indeed alarming for physical-store owners. These statistics often make pundits fuss hysterically, making them claim that the age of brick-and-mortar retail is almost dead. As a matter of fact, they are dead wrong!

Brick-and-mortar stores in the US have been valued at $4 trillion last year. Does this imply that the brick-and-mortar stores are too big to give in? Definitely not.

Just walk through majority of the stores, and you will find various inefficiencies and inconsistencies. However, a fundamental transformation is taking place at grass roots as managers and business owners engage in trying to fulfil the changing needs of the consumers.

The consumers of today are mobile, digital, and physical in the sense that they expect to see retailers wherever they are. Hence, physical-store retailers should be willing to adapt to technologies, merchandising, and pricing to match the consumers' desires to carry out research and make a purchase as they please.

This transformation heavily depends on understanding not only the needs and wants of the customers but also their actual movement within the store. The analysis of such data can reveal both the plus points of your store as well as its negative aspects. Where do customers go when they first enter the store? Which area do they spend the most time in? How long does it take them to check out? All these questions can be easily and accurately answered through the implementation of latest technologies, including Wi-Fi tracking, which allows store owners to monitor the movement of their customers as well as their employees to maximise sales, store efficiency, and customer service.

WHAT WILL YOU FIND IN THIS BOOK?

This book covers numerous aspects of retailing, with the ultimate aim of highlighting the Wi-Fi tracking technology and its benefits for the retail industry.

The book starts with an introduction to retailing, which gives an overview of the retail industry.

As it is already clear, the consumer of today has transformed and become more demanding, and it has become imperative for retailers to understand how and what the new consumer expects of them. This is covered in the second chapter of this book.

The third chapter focuses on the rise of e-commerce and how it has affected brick-and-mortar stores, while the fourth chapter discusses why analytical data is of great importance for physical stores.

Learn how to harness the power of information in the fifth chapter of this book, '**When Big Data Meets Business Analytics**'.

We then move on to discuss how this data can be used to make smart business decisions that contribute to an increase in the operational efficiency of the store. To properly bridge the gap between physical and online stores, it is important to understand the differences between them—chapter 7 talks precisely about this gap.

Last but not the least, chapters 9 and 10 focus on how IT solutions, particularly the Wi-Fi tracking solutions, can help a business grow.

It is hoped that this book will be of great importance to all those who are involved in the retail industry.

SYNOPSIS

The retail landscape is in a continuous transition as it faces strong headwinds as a result of rapidly changing consumer behaviour, which is driven by the immense impact of e-commerce and the Internet. The growing popularity of e-commerce channels and the increasing use of devices such as smartphones and tablets for shopping have provided consumers multiple ways of fulfilling their shopping needs, which were previously limited to brick-and-mortar stores prior to the advent of the Internet.

This impact has caused many retail stores to shut their doors, including retail giants, which have been forced to reduce the number of physical stores. These changes have made many retail store owners to ponder ways that they can strengthen their position in the midst of these unstoppable changes.

The consumers of today are much more knowledgeable, have more options, and are now at the helm of the retail industry as they steer through a myriad of technological advances and developments made available for them.

Even though e-commerce has had a huge impact on the sales and the bottom line of brick-and-mortar stores, it is fortunate to see that many wise retailers are beginning to understand what it takes to attract customers despite the transformation.

The fact that online shopping websites and portals have had an edge over retail stores in terms of the analytical tools available at their disposal cannot be denied. The former, right from its inception, has had certain techniques to learn about the habits of their customers and has used it to their advantage by offering and suggesting products and services based on the behaviour of the consumers. For many years, technology has been on their side.

Fortunately, the technology and technique to assist brick-and-mortar stores to better understand consumer behaviour have emerged, and many retailers have already implemented such tools, with more of them understanding the need to do so.

These tools we speak of have enabled these stores to gather precious analytics that they can use to understand the shopping trends and behaviour of consumers while using these to make smart business decisions. Leveraging IT solutions has become more of a necessity than a luxury for them as the competition between offline and online stores continues to rage with all its might.

This book sheds light on crucial topics to help brick-and-mortar business owners and decision makers to better understand the direction that the retail industry needs to take in order to minimise and eliminate the effects of their online counterparts.

In fact, if proper steps are taken and the right technology is implemented, brick-and-mortar stores will have a higher chance of generating greater sales, primarily due to the trust factor they can induce in people.

CHAPTER 1: INTRODUCTION
TO RETAILING

Retailing is undoubtedly among one of the rapidly growing segments of our economy. It is also among one of the largest employers and provides superb business opportunities to those who seek it. It is estimated that around 12 per cent of the 750,000 new businesses launched between the years 2001 and 2002 belongs to the retail industry. The entrepreneurs behind such ventures earn a living by investing their capital and time by offering consumers things they need.

The majority of retailing requires an entrepreneur to buy merchandise or a certain service from manufacturers, agents, wholesalers, an importer, or perhaps, even another retailer and then sell that product or service to consumers. The prices these retailers charge for offering the products or services not only cover the retailers' expenses but also provide them a profit (in an ideal situation, that is).

Each year, the retailing industry accounts for around two-thirds of all the economic activities in the US. The National Retail Federation (NRF), in 2005, reported that the entire retail sales in the United States had reached the $4.1 trillion mark in year 2004.

There are all kinds of storefront ventures, ranging from health food to clothing boutiques to coffee shops, Laundromats, bars, and convenience stores to hardware stores and more. One of the latest arrivals in the retail industry are the pop-up retailers and shops, which are basically set up for only a couple of days or weeks at a given time, including many of the holiday stores that you may have seen during Halloween or Christmas.

According to NRF, the numbers of retail establishments in the US are in excess of 1.5 million stores/shops. Most of these are brick-and-mortar stores; however, there are many other types of retailers present, such as e-commerce (also known as e-tailing), automatic merchandising (vending machines), or direct retailing (door-to-door selling), along with many service providers.

To date, the retail and service sectors in the US economy keep on reporting the greatest number of start-up businesses.

What about the Jobs?

According to the NRF, there are more than forty-two million workers in the US who belong to the retailing industry. In other words, one individual out of every four people works in the retailing industry. Presently, there are more jobs in retailing than in the entire manufacturing sector in the US. Also according to the NRF, 13 per cent of all new jobs created in the US are in the retailing industry.

Types of Retailers

Retailing is considered to be one of the most mature industries in the US economy and continues to be reinvented as the industry takes advantage of new technology. The ever-changing attitudes, behaviours, and buying patterns as well as the restructuring of the industry itself have resulted in a huge impact on start-up businesses. Even though some predictions state that the local retailer may become extinct, there is indeed a promising future for all those who adapt to the changing needs of consumers as rapidly and as efficiently as possible, especially if they can do this far better than their larger contenders can. With TV, Internet, overnight delivery, telephone, and debit and credit cards, any individual with some enterprising flair can choose a niche and start conducting commercial transactions immediately.

To provide you with an accurate overview of today's competitive marketplace, we will look at the various types of retailers presently offering the needs of customers. Do not forget the fact that almost all of today's large enterprises have started off with nothing but a simple concept and that they have grown to such large sizes due to their patience, perseverance, and ability to **adapt to the changing needs of their customers.**

Store Retailing

With an abundance of department stores, independent shops, off-price and discount enterprises, convenience stores, national/regional chains, supermarkets, and various other large-scale enterprises, the retail scene in America is astounding.

Such retailers run point-of-sale sites that attract an increasingly high volume of customers (walk-in). These stores typically utilise extensive merchandise displays as well as mass media advertising techniques to draw the attention of customers.

The types of products they offer are normally targeted to the general public for their everyday personal/household consumption. However, many of these stores also target institutional and business clients, offering things such as computer hardware and software, office supplies, building materials, electrical and plumbing supplies, and more.

The US Census Bureau treats catalogue showrooms, automotive dealers, gasoline service stations, and mobile home dealers as retail stores.

Brick-and-Mortar Stores

Even though Internet shopping has transformed much of the retail landscape, independent brick-and-mortar stores continue to lead consumer sales and are expected to continue to do so, provided that certain measures are taken to adapt to the needs of consumers. One of the reasons behind the success of brick-and-mortar stores is their real-world presence. A physical location lends solid credibility and makes a certain store appear reliable. It provides a gathering place, an outlet, and a destination for customers. One-on-one exchanges and shared experiences are appreciated by individuals of all ages. To the human nature, the ability to look at someone and ask questions or watch demonstrations offers immense appeal.

Another advantage is that being able to smell and feel the product prior to purchasing it provides shoppers a realistic comparison with other similar products. There is also the gratification of carrying the new product home with them. That there are no packing and shipping charges adds to the appeal of shopping at brick-and-mortar stores. Returning any items to the store is much more convenient than mailing them back.

Also, personal service, local employment, and community involvement are some of the things that will persist on making these stores appealing to the public for many years to come. However, the fact that e-commerce platforms are increasingly adapting to the needs of consumers and providing them an ever-increasing personalised service cannot be denied, and unless brick-and-mortar stores adapt to the latest technologies to better understand and serve their customers, the latter will experience serious problems as the competition grows.

David versus Goliath

Power retailers such as Home Depot, Walmart, and Target are known to almost everyone. With their huge facilities and a wide range of products offered, these price-oriented giants are likely to crush every other little start-up on the horizon, right? Not necessarily.

Many of the new 'Davids' are now learning the tricks from the 'Goliaths' and are now slowly yet steadily flexing their muscles. As a matter of fact, the US is a nation consisting of a greater number of small merchants.

A typical store is operated by an owner alone or by a team of husband and wife. Naturally, such stores lack the resources, sophisticated operations, and purchasing muscle of the Goliath stores. These small retailers may only employ one or two workers. However, the store's size is dependent upon the type of business it conducts. For instance, a furniture store requires more space compared to a neighbourhood grocery store.

Specialty Retailing

Power retailers such as Walmart and Home Depot sell the 'needs', whereas specialty retailers focus on offering the 'wants'. The latter focuses on neighbourhood convenience, how rich the shopping experience is, and that the inventory meets their target customers' needs on a more personalised basis.

In this type of retailing, small stores display surprising resilience and strength in the face of competition from larger retailers as well as retailers that are based on the Internet. This is mainly because they offer the customer a much warmer atmosphere; perhaps this, coupled with a greater selection of available merchandise, adds to the shopping experience. When compared to manufacturing operations, these types of retail outlets are much easier to start with both in terms of the finances and the operations. Nevertheless, undercapitalization, insufficient market analysis, and poor location have been the most common reasons behind the failure of such stores.

Nonstore Retailing

A discussion on the types of retail outlets will be incomplete without mention of the $172 billion nonstore retail sector. Such businesses are mainly engaged in selling products through electronic shopping, TV, electronic catalogues, paper, in-home demonstrations, vending machines, portable stalls, door-to-door solicitation, and mail order.

With the exclusion of vending, such businesses don't always keep a stock for sale on the exact premises, with most of them dealing in coins, books, magazines, jewellery, audiotapes, stamps, novelty merchandise, CDs, and numerous other home shopping endeavours.

The Internet

Ever since the emergence of e-commerce platforms that allow people to shop over the Internet, the entire retailing landscape has been changed for good. The Internet has connected businesses, markets, and consumers together. According to statistics, online sales in the US account for only 6.7 per cent of all retail sales, which turns out to be just around $300 billion of a multitrillion-dollar industry.

Online sales have had a huge impact on the way consumers can search for and make purchasing decisions. Using the Internet, consumers can easily compare prices, compare products, and perform extensive research before buying them. Many online platforms are now providing their customers a personalised shopping experience by recommending products that they are most likely to buy, based on any purchases that they have made in the past. This goes a long way in providing the customers with a rich shopping experience, which has previously been an integral part of the way specialty retailers have done business.

All kinds of storefront retailers are now utilizing the Internet to their advantage by augmenting their sales by **adapting to the needs of customers.**

The Image of Retailers

In the retail industry, the secret to success lies in customer satisfaction. Retail businesses exist with a sole reason: to make their customers happy. The extent to which these businesses succeed in making their customers happy depends on how much it is willing to grow. This industry is continuously shifting its image from one that generates profits from other people to one that strives to serve the interests of others. Image, as we speak, has many facets, including
- friendliness of the staff employed by the business,
- quality of merchandise,
- level of service, and
- ease of access.

You, as an entrepreneur, need to be aware of the perceived risks that the consumer has when doing business with your company. The first is the **social risk:** *what a person buys affects how other people view him/her*—smart and fashionable or ignorant and behind the times.

The second is the **economic risk.** This is when the possibility that individuals' purchasing decisions significantly reduce their budget while not yielding enough value or satisfaction.

Social Responsibility

Retailers nowadays tend to enhance their image by taking on greater social responsibility. By doing this, they meet the needs of the entire society as a whole instead of just trying to boost their profits and bottom line. These businesses often provide their own facilities for forums, art exhibits, and numerous types of community activities. Even large retailers get involved in fulfilling their social responsibility, with their executives leading fundraising campaigns to benefit the community and hosting programs, sponsoring events, and mentoring students.

As a business owner, you will have many opportunities to get involved in things that matter to your customers.

Many retailers even prefer to relocate to an area that has been wrecked over the years. Utilizing some of their profits, they supplement federal funds to revive the area. However, locating in such areas poses certain challenges and risks, including shoplifting, vandalism, and other types of crimes. Nevertheless, many retailers are determined to improve these areas by playing their part in upgrading them.

RANDOM FACT

Retailers' Call to Action

To fight the problems associated with sweatshops, all the members of the United States' National Retail Federation (NRF) have to endorse the *Statement of Principles on Supplier Legal Compliance* while pledging that they
- are dedicated to ethical business practices and legal compliance,
- choose only those suppliers who are committed to the same principles,
- include contractual language necessitating their suppliers to follow the law,
- take correct action if their supplier violates the law, and
- support and cooperate with law enforcement agencies in the correct implementation of their responsibilities.

Tracy Mullin, the former president of NRF, said in this regard:

'Retailers take their responsibilities to their customers very seriously, and we have taken aggressive and proactive steps to help our suppliers obey the law. Retailers have answered the call and are doing their part to ensure that the products they sell are made legally, ethically and morally.'

Windows of Opportunity for Retailers

In today's retail industry, offering a product or service and marketing it are no longer a guarantee that a retail firm will expand and succeed. As a business owner, you have to ensure that you keep a constant eye on the changing needs of the consumer. There must be a present strategic view of your company, and you must focus on positioning and transforming consumer lifestyles as well as on technological advances in general.

Out of all the habits of successful enterprises that are involved in selling directly to the consumer, the ability to review relationships with the marketplace is probably the most important. The ability to anticipate and then adapt to the constant flux in retail environment more rapidly than the competitor is what makes these businesses successful. These business owners harness the power of change to become more innovative, growth-intensive, energetic, and profitable ones, and these things are exactly what distinguish them from static failures.

The Rise of Online Businesses and Their Impact on Brick-and-Mortar Stores

Even though we have learned that physical stores offer a lot of advantages over online businesses in many areas, these physical stores have been in crisis for the past few years. During the shopping season in 2013, such retailers have seen only half the foot traffic they have experienced just three years back, according to statistics by *ShopperTrak*.

With the confidence of consumers growing significantly, the reduction in foot traffic indicates a tectonic shift in the consumers' way of shopping and buying.

Modern consumers lead very busy lives, and shopping is something that takes time. For some, it is a task. An increasing number of consumers find it more convenient to research and shop on the Internet than visit brick-and-mortar stores. While in-store incursions can be very enjoyable, for a lot of people, shopping online or using their mobile device is something that gives them a far more enjoyable experience.

In many cases, these customers have access to a greater amount of information than they can get from a sales associate at a physical store. Online reviews and cost comparison tools make them feel as if they have more control over the purchase and their buying decision in general.

As Online and Mobile Shopping Grow

The trend of online shopping continues to grow as more and more people enjoy the convenience offered by the Internet. ComScore, an Internet analytics company, has reported a 10 per cent increase in online purchases throughout the holiday shopping season of 2013, and it will be safe to say that this has continued to increase as time has gone by.

> **RANDOM FACT**
> Trust is a major issue that influences consumers' purchasing decisions. Despite the increasing number of people purchasing online, there are still many people who simply do not trust online vendors.
>
> These consumers have greater trust for brick-and-mortar stores due to the physical presence of such retailers.

Amazon, the famous online retailer, has stated that in 2013, over 36.8 million items have been purchased worldwide—and that too on Cyber Monday alone! Amazon continues to establish its online empire with much momentum.

Today's consumers have increased expectations, with almost 71 per cent of them expecting to see an in-store inventory online. On the other hand, 50 per cent of consumers want the option of purchasing online as well as an option that allows them to pick up the product in-store.

With the advent of smartphones, this trend has escalated further as many online retailers have developed their own applications (as well as responsive websites) that allow people to buy easily using their mobile phones, regardless of whether they are at work, at home, or on the go.

A recent study by Forrester Research[1] indicates that 56 per cent of consumers have used their mobile phones or tablets to research products when at home, 38 per cent of people have used a device to check the availability of a product while on the way to a store, and 34 per cent of consumers have used their devices to perform research while in the store.

What Does This Mean for Brick-and-Mortar Retailers?

It is good to know that brick-and-mortar retailers are not entirely blind to these consumer trends. The word *omnichannel* has been on the lips of everyone who has visited a recently held conference by the National Retail Federation in New York.

Omnichannel is the concept that each and every channel has to work together in order to deliver a consistent and unified customer experience.

The problem, however, lies with the term *omnichannel* still containing the word *channel*. Many retailers assume this requires them to be able to offer in-store pickups of orders placed online or accept returns in-store of orders placed on the Internet. The solution extends beyond such initiatives in order to be able to satisfy even the most basic needs of today's consumers. The use of omnichannel methods boils down to achieving the following:

- Increasing lifetime value of consumers
- Creating higher margins by reducing markdowns of stocks stuck at wrong stores
- Delivering faster inventory turns
- Providing the customers an enriched shopping experience

Other groups of retailers, while aware of the term *omnichannel,* do not seem interested enough to take a further glance into what it is and what they should be doing to keep up with the intense competition posed by online retailers. We cannot forget the fact that many huge retailers, such as Best Buy, have been forced to shutter many of their stores around the country.

This should be enough to ring bells in the minds of small-business owners.

---

1 *'Customer Desires Vs. Retailer Capabilities: Minding the Omni-Channel Commerce Gap', Forrester Research, SOURCE.*

CHAPTER 2: GETTING TO KNOW THE NEW CONSUMER

Some of the questions that must be asked by all types of businesses—retail or online—are the following:

- Do you really know who your customers are?
- Do you know how they purchase their products or services?
- Do they know the options available for them to make this transaction?

The retailers who know the consumer and apply what they know are the ones that have a competitive advantage in their respective industries. They understand that regardless of whether a customer makes a purchase or not, they leave footprints. These footprints are created in a number of ways, including when potential customers

- browse a business's website,
- perform mobile searches,
- contact its call centre,
- question in-store staff,
- answer surveys, and
- make purchases.

The footprints that **consumers** leave behind leave many clues about **them**, including information such as who the customers

> **RANDOM FACT**
>
> The modern consumer is much harder to impress. Gone are the days when all retailers have to do is present a product, stating how superb it is.
>
> Now, retailers have to prove to the consumer that the product has been made for them.

are, what has influenced them, what they are interested in buying, how often they buy, where they shop, and a lot of other information.

Just like detectives rely heavily on their collection of evidence, companies need to focus on gathering and using business analytics to better understand their customers. This knowledge is then used to reach conclusions and make crucial decisions.

Just think about it: if you have sufficient information about who your customers are, you will be in a better position to offer them what they are looking for and thereby gain a competitive edge over your rivals. Many of these clues are simply what the customer is trying to tell you!

Twenty-First-Century Retailing

The twenty-first century has introduced numerous forms of digital communication to the point that it has become a norm for today's consumers. This—coupled with the swift development of various technologies and huge quantities, types, and speed of data today's consumers create—has affected almost every industry; however, the effects are far more prominent on the retail industry.

> **RANDOM TIP**
> In the twenty-first-century retailing industry, it's the survival of the fittest. If you want your business to stand a chance of surviving the intense competition, you will have to **adapt.**
>
> Adapt to the needs of the customers, build loyalty, and take every step possible to know them.

Just focus on this for a moment. Since the advent of social media, there has been a platform available to suit every other niche. Product reviews available online as well as recommendations through word-of-mouth marketing are widespread, and the reach is global. Mobile devices have grown rapidly in numbers and have totally altered the retail landscape by providing consumers utmost convenience and flexibility. Apart from this, all kinds of new purchasing channels are opening up, resulting in an empowered and well-informed consumer who now has much higher expectations and demands from businesses.

As a result of all this, it has become more complex for retailers to precisely understand the behaviour of their customers as well as their purchasing patterns. It has become more challenging for businesses to develop important customer segments, optimise delivery, predict demand, drive profitability, and protect margins. To make things even more difficult, the consumers have begun to demand a flawless experience from businesses, regardless of the way they make a purchase from them. This has made all processes related to customer attainment, growth, and retention more vital and more convoluted.

Getting to Know the Modern Consumers

The IBM Institute for Business Value has outlined three unique characteristics of twenty-first century's modern consumers.

The Consumers Are Instrumented

With emerging technologies such as mobile devices, Internet, in-store technologies, and others, today's consumers now have immediate access to huge amounts of information about products, services, and retailers.

The consumers now use this information to make purchasing decisions, including carefully reviewing the performance of a product, comparing prices—and value for many—and many other

> **RANDOM FACT**
> Over five hundred million mobile devices belong to people who do not even have electricity in their homes and depend on village charging stations or solar power to charge their devices.
>
> This is how much mobile devices have penetrated into all kinds of societies.

aspects related to their products. They also search for the best deals and have many options to choose from when it comes to the payment methods and delivery options available to them.

For example, in a few clicks, consumers can place an order for an item that is delivered right to their doorstep. On the other hand, they may research online but prefer to buy the product in-store after physically reviewing it too. In a nutshell, the options are virtually unlimited for consumers.

Younger consumers are swifter in embracing the latest technology as it provides them a greater sense of control over their purchase. This is more common in emerging markets, where there weren't as many shopping choices previously, as have become available with the up-and-coming technologies.

Despite the growth in technologies and online shopping experiences, the focus cannot shift entirely from brick-and-mortar stores to digital, online ones. We cannot ignore the fact that a huge number of people use their mobile devices to search for physical stores where they can buy a product in person—not all use their devices to buy online!

Some use their devices to check inventory for the availability of their desired items at the store before they actually visit it. Regardless of how much technology has penetrated our lives, brick-and-mortar stores remain to be the primary channel of purchase for consumers, and adaptive retailers are leveraging the power of technology to serve instrumented consumers and provide them a more seamless buying experience.

We will talk about how brick-and-mortar store owners are using technology to their advantage later in this book.

The Consumers Are More Interconnected

There has been a radical change in how consumers learn about products and different retailers. There was a time when retailers were the primary (only, in many cases) source of information about their physical stores and the products available.

Today, consumers have very slight reliance on retailers for information. This is because the Internet has connected millions of people together from all over the world who share product reviews and comments on the products.

Putting this in other words, modern consumers listen more to other consumers compared to the retailers. Consumers now have strong influence on others right from the very start of the purchase's decision-making process.

Out of all the people who were part of IBM's polls, one-third were likely to 'follow' a particular retailer on their social media page to get to try new products or get preferential treatment. However, the same number of consumers would also depend on other consumers to get the information about the quality of products and services from the retailer.

As time passes, this phenomenon is expected to grow further. The population of the world has been predicted to grow by 12 per cent over the next ten years by the UN census data. An increasing number of people live in

> ### RANDOM FACT
> Today's shoppers want to feel powerful and want to have a semblance of control over their purchases.
>
> Retailers can make them feel as such by offering various options for their shopping needs. For instance, one of the most effective ways to achieve this is by offering omnichannel methods—that is, an option for your consumers to check stocks and read product reviews, descriptions, and other information right on your website even before they visit your store.

urban areas compared to rural localities, and more than half of the population of the emerging world fall into the category of middle class by the standards of their own countries. The result is a bigger pool of more diverse, prosperous, and technology-savvy individuals—not to mention more demanding!

Modern Consumers Are Much More Intelligent

Besides becoming more instrumented and more interconnected, the modern consumers have also grown to become more intelligent about the way they implement technology in their lives for the purpose of smarter shopping. These consumers have clearly established ideas regarding their needs, and they have clear expectations from the retailers.

The IBM study has utilised the *MaxDiff analysis,* in which the respondents have compared varying attributes—similar to the way they do when they shop in real life—to spot things that matter the most to them when they shop, including the areas they want retailers to improve upon. IBM has found out that modern consumers have a strong belief that retailers should have greater focus on providing better promotions as well as prices, and they should continuously improve the standards of their products.

More precisely, consumers wish to gain personalised discounts and a consistently available stock of products. They also demand better quality, value, and variety.

Almost two-thirds of the participants of the poll have stated that they are willing to spend more with the retailer that listens to their suggestions regarding improvements and provides a personalised brand experience.

How to Adapt to the Modern Consumer

As we've previously mentioned, in today's industries, only the fittest companies can survive the intense competition. This survival is only possible if the retailer adapts to the changing circumstances. There is no denying the fact that the retailers who continuously refine their marketing, sales, and overall business strategies to adapt to the needs of consumers and implement emerging technologies are the ones that succeed. Such businesses show increasing profit margins quarter after quarter.

To deal with such challenges as well as opportunities, attention needs to be focused on business analytics, which is not exactly a theory that has been executed by ancient statisticians. In fact, it's a crucial business tool that applies to the entire organization's decision makers. The ultimate aim of every business is to meet the needs of its customers and increase customer loyalty; hence, all the decisions need to be made accordingly in the light of accurate business analytics.

Business analytics helps businesses and retailers adapt with the modern consumers in numerous ways:

RANDOM FACT
Offering consumers a unified brand experience is dependent on the way you have aligned your customer strategy and the access of information throughout the whole retail organization.

This is no less than a challenge; however, it's something that pays off well in the long run.

- Analysing the customers' behaviour, sentiment, and buying patterns then responding to the needs of the individuals
- Delivering products and personalised promotions at the right time for the right products in the

consumers' preferred way of purchase to encourage them to buy
- Precisely predicting the demand to properly protect margins, optimise assortment, and eventually, drive profitability
- Creating a unique brand experience to enhance loyalty of customers, keeping in mind the omnichannel approach that numerous consumers use to research and buy products
- Gathering the information about and analysing the influencing factors of the consumers while understanding how these factors affect the purchasing decisions of the customers

The new retail realities of today are not only transforming the way companies conduct business, but they are also having a significant impact on the way retail organizations are being structured and the areas where the investments are being targeted. For instance, in silos, running channels tend to be much more expensive for the retailers, and it also does not meet the needs of an omnichannel customer who is persistent on getting a consistent brand experience regardless if they shop online, at a kiosk, using a mobile phone or tablet, or at a physical store.

The Shopping Process

The purchase of every product nowadays is a result of a fairly complex shopping process, which starts off with discovering the product, testing it, pickup or delivery, and in many instances, to returns. The modern-day, technology-savvy consumers have a crystal clear idea of what they want, including
- price,
- style, and
- availability of the product.

While having a greater awareness of their needs as well as the options that they have, the consumers of today also focus on enjoying an engaging shopping experience. With so many options available where consumers can get their desired product, loyalty often runs short. Brick-and-mortar retailers have to adapt to these changing circumstances and implement the necessary technologies to serve these savvy consumers if they are to gain an edge over their competitors, online and offline alike.

Transformation of the Purchase Cycle

Gone are the days when customers enter a store and are greeted by a salesperson that often ends up selling a product. In those days, the consumers do not have as many options as they do now, nor do they have access to information and deals in just a few clicks.

Consumers choose a channel after considering a wide range of criteria, ranging from brand loyalty to physical convenience to the ultimate desire to be surprised or entertained. Thus, where and how customer value is created and how it is captured solely depend on the preferences of a consumer. Nonetheless, a study has revealed that, irrespective of the preferences of the consumers, brick-and-mortar stores remain the cornerstone of this purchase cycle, which comprises of several steps before an actual purchase takes place.

The buying process starts and involves the following locations:

1. **At Home**

The consumer, when intending to buy a certain product, begins the buying process at home by doing the following:
- Searching online
- Browsing reviews
- Creating wish lists
- Liking companies and products on social media
- Receiving coupons or offers

2. To the Store

When on the way to a store, or when roaming around in a mall, consumers use their smartphones to do the following:

- ▸ Locate a store
- ▸ Read product reviews
- ▸ Look at their wish list
- ▸ Receive coupons

3. In the Store

Statistics indicate that as many as 79 per cent of consumers use their smartphones while inside a store for the following purposes:

- ▸ Searching for prices online
- ▸ Showrooming
- ▸ Utilizing loyalty apps
- ▸ Receiving gamification offers and coupons
- ▸ Texting and chatting

4. At the Shelf/Rack

When at a particular shelf or rack where their desired product is located, they may use the digital kiosks for more information, to sign up for offers, to order products to be shipped, and to get help.

5. Upon Purchase

At checkout, consumers can use their smartphones to do the following:

- ▸ Redeem an offer
- ▸ Register their purchase on loyalty app
- ▸ Earn loyalty points

6. Back at Home

After returning home, the vendor can follow up the individuals, offer them coupons, ask for product reviews if the consumer has purchased a product from them, and carry out targeted advertising.

This, however, will depend on how the vendor has implemented technology and whether or not the retailer focuses on omnichannel marketing techniques.

CHAPTER 3: THE RISE OF E-COMMERCE

Nonstore retail has, for quite some time, been a major business feature. Flyers and catalogues have generated a lot of sales, and still do, along with TV programs, such as those on the Home Shopping Network. The elephant, however, is the B2C e-commerce, which has rapidly surpassed all other types of nonstore retail.

The Requirement for Retail Space

The demand for any retail space is dependent upon the money that consumers possess for retail expenditures, along with the actual productivity levels of the retail space. In addition, the demand for retail space can also be influenced greatly by purchases made on credit; however, North American consumers' debt is already at an all-time high. Future-met increases in the demand for total retail space will depend upon increases in income and population growth.

Increases in income are, however, little to none, meaning that the primary factor will be population growth.

Once a certain item is purchased through e-commerce and then delivered from the wholesaler or manufacturer to the consumer's home, the latter does not have to visit the store. As a result, the physical store loses relevancy, reducing its need for extra space or, in the worst case, requiring no space at all.

A growing number of retailers are adopting e-commerce solutions to enhance the services offered to their customers using Internet kiosks within the physical stores. These solutions have enabled retailers (even brick-and-mortar ones) to enter international markets and improve their overall service provision.

Omnichannel and multichannel retailing are the famous buzzwords these days even though increasing quantities of products and services are acquired over the Internet. Initially, the numbers of sales on the Internet have been quite limited, with books, travel, video, banking, and software being the most common products or services available through it.

While there are some exceptions that continue, including dry-cleaning services, haircuts, gourmet restaurant meals, and the like, there has been a steady rise of retailers offering purchases through the Internet.

The consumer can utilise the Internet to learn about a certain product's reliability, availability, and reputation and compare prices right from the comfort of their homes. Showrooming is one aspect of comparison shopping in which the consumers analyse a product in-store but purchase it online, forcing brick-and-mortar retailers to match prices with that of online stores. This has a direct impact on survivability.

Many retailers have suspended their operations, while many others are reducing the number of their stores or their store sizes. A few examples of stores closing in the US back in 2013 as a result of e-commerce include the following:

- Barnes & Noble—closed up to 240 out of 689 stores
- Best Buy—closed up to 250 out of 1,056 stores
- Office Depot—closed up to 150 out of 1,114 stores
- Sears Holdings—closed up to 125 Sears as well as 225 Kmart units out of a total of 2,118

Besides the above, there are many other stores that have had to face the same fate as a result of the rise of e-commerce. In a Toronto-based newspaper, *The Globe and Mail,* it was published that Staples was planning to close down 40 of its stores in Canada partially because of the effects of e-commerce. Best Buy in Canada was planning to close 15 of its 230 stores for similar reasons. It is a fact that these large retail stores used to offer the best prices in a number of retail categories; however, the Internet has had a huge impact on them.

Many of the retailers are even reducing the sizes of their stores, while some, such as Old Navy, are turning towards franchising. For some, smaller units that resemble more of a showroom than a store are becoming a much more feasible option; on the other hand, some stores are simply not building any more stores like they have done in the past. Marks & Spencer has announced in 2013 that it will cease building any additional stores in the UK. It will be interesting to know that UK has one of the highest penetration rates of e-commerce.

The Positive Side

Fortunately, in US and Canada, a lot of existing shopping malls are being upgraded and modernised even though very little new projects are being planned. In some markets, new retailers are emerging, while existing ones are increasing efficiency or 'going green'. Retailing in North America is far from being dead, as revealed by the statistics we have discussed previously.

Size of E-Commerce

In 2012, total e-commerce sales in the US have reached $225.3 billion, around 16 per cent more than the numbers in 2011. In comparison, retail sales have only increased by 5 per cent from the year 2011 to 2012.

An American market research firm, Forrester Research, projects that e-commerce sales in the US will reach $370 billion by 2017,[2] which represents 10 per cent of the total retail sales. However, experts believe that if brick-and-mortar stores will take the necessary steps and adopt technology to compete with e-commerce stores and understand the changing needs of consumers, the stores can grow rapidly.

---

2 *'US Ecommerce Sales to Hit $370B by 2017, fueled by Mobile', Forrester Research, SOURCE.*

CHAPTER 4: IMPORTANCE OF ANALYTICS FOR RETAIL

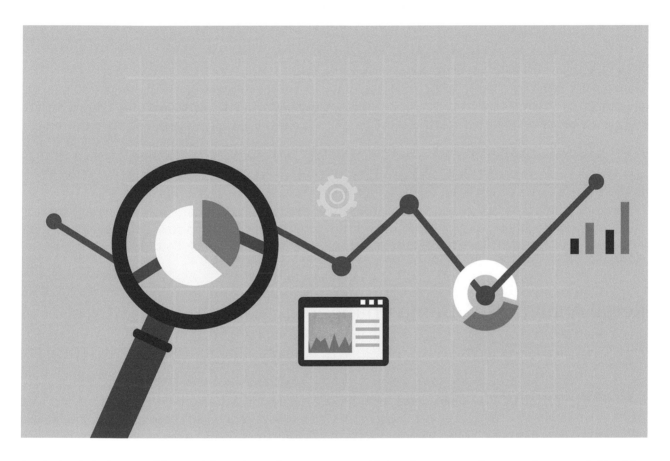

Analytics is being used for a wide variety of purposes, and it has become an immensely powerful tool for retailers. With the transforming retailing landscape, it has become essential for brick-and-mortar stores to gather and use analytical data to their advantage.

E-commerce has always been at the forefront of analytics, collecting and gathering all kinds of data regarding the modern customers and giving online retailers an opportunity to meet their growing demands and changing needs. Unfortunately, the retail industry has been slow in collecting and analysing such data for the purpose of enhancing the consumers' experience.

As e-commerce increases steadily, many stores have been forced to close down or reduce their size. Numerous other changes in the way people buy products have also influenced this, including the concept of showrooming.

In this chapter, we will discuss why analytics is important and how retailers can benefit from it.

The Opportunities and Challenges

The opportunity presented to retailers from analytics is simply enormous. Using various analytical tools, retailers of brick-and-mortar stores can

- strive to develop stronger relationships with customers based on a clear understanding of their needs and behaviour;
- deliver targeted promotions, advertising, and offers to consumers to motivate them to make a purchase;
- balance the inventory with the demand so the stores are never out of stock or carry any excess inventory;
- charge prices that customers are ready to pay; and
- figure out the ideal use of marketing investments.

Many leading firms are already taking great advantage of analytics. For instance, Kroger gets 40 per cent redemption rate from its coupons, which are analytically targeted. This is huge, compared to an industry average of a mere 2 per cent. Kroger believes that these promotions have increased its overall sales by 5 per cent.

CVS uses analytics to target the coupons at its POS, believing in its analytical capability as a mammoth profit centre.

However, majority of retailers still find it difficult to digest all the technology, the data, and the analytics that can be made available to them. Many of them simply do not understand how to implement an analytics solution, let alone use it. Many don't have the skill to assist themselves in improving their bottom line, while many are simply not comfortable with the strategies built around analytical capabilities.

Retail Analytics—A Game Changer

By utilizing analytics tools, retailers can enhance customer loyalty by giving the consumers a more personalised experience.

In today's markets, where an economic uncertainty prevails, retailers have to improve their approach of driving traffic as well as sales. With an ever-increasing mobility, the always-connected shopper of today is capable of carrying out research even when he or she is standing inside the store. As a result of such flexibility and abundance of options, brand loyalty has been seriously affected. Consumers can now shift brands quickly, depending on the availability of products, the price, and the opinions of other shoppers.

We cannot forget the impact of social media, where users are increasingly likely to report their experience of using a certain brand. As a result of these trends, it has definitely become more difficult for retailers to increase customer traffic along with customer loyalty. Many retailers now realise that loyalty programs now need to go well beyond the mere points, rewards, and discounts and move towards developing a personalised shopping experience for the consumer. This personalised treatment has to be based on the individual customer's needs and behaviour. All this can only be achieved with the help of analytics.

The Importance of Customer Loyalty

Established retailers know that the only way to succeed in today's dynamic markets is to find new ways of attracting new customers and boosting the loyalty of the existing customer base. The term *loyalty* in today's market means transforming a first-time customer into a repeat one and, eventually, to a brand advocate.

The following pieces of research emphasise how important customer loyalty is for businesses, particularly the brick-and-mortar stores, which are facing the challenge of keeping themselves up to date with the changing consumer demands.

- It has been found that acquiring new customers costs up to five times more than it does retaining existing customers.[3]
- Customer profitability rates usually increase over the life of a customer who has been retained. Reducing churn by as little as 5 per cent can increase the profits from 25 per cent to a staggering 125 per cent.
- The chances of selling a product or service to an existing customer are between 60 and 70 per cent, whereas the probability is between 5 and 20 per cent for a new prospect.
- As much as 70 per cent of the identified reasons why customers usually leave a company have nothing to do with the product at all. In fact, the main reason behind the switch is poor quality of service.

> **RANDOM FACT**
> It is cheaper for a business to retain repeat customers than to draw in new customers.
>
> Repeat customers are a symbol of loyalty and can turn out to become brand advocates, thereby marketing your products and services through powerful word-of-mouth marketing.

It is important to understand that good customer service can only be provided to the customer if the company understands his or her need in the first place. Online shopping websites are capable of gathering huge amounts of data by monitoring what products the user browses through, and it suggests similar products accordingly. This can be seen in practice at Amazon, where there are suggestions at the bottom page of the product you are already viewing. This gives the user the impression that he or she is being understood—a powerful factor for inducing loyalty.

Getting back to retail stores, there are numerous ways of gathering analytical data, with new, emerging technologies such as Wi-Fi tracking, which we will be discussing in the coming chapters.

Analytics in Customer Loyalty

Analytics refers to the science of analysing and then discovering meaningful patterns in the data. Analytics tools can assist retailers and allow them to connect to the customers at every point of the life cycle by turning the patterns into useful and valuable insights that appear to not only describe but also predict business performance.

Two of the most common types of analytics that are used by today's businesses are as follows:
- **Predictive models**—These models analyse the past performance of the business to calculate the likelihood that a consumer will exhibit a particular type of behaviour in order to enhance marketing effectiveness. This allows the business to predict customer reactions to a certain product and can be used to improve the basket size, increase the value of the basket, and switch the consumer to a much better and profitable offer.
- **Descriptive models**—Descriptive models are known for quantifying relationships in the data and classifying prospects and customers into groups. Unlike the previous type, which only focuses on the behaviour of a single consumer, descriptive models effectively identify the product-customer relationship.

Retailers can take advantage of these models and turn traditional retail into analytical retail.

---

3 *'In Search of Customer Loyalty', the Insight Advantage, SOURCE.*

With analytics tools, retailers can easily
- spot their most profitable target consumer base through profiling and customer segmentation and
- develop relationships with customers based on a deeper understanding of their behaviour and needs while predicting future behaviour.

The Span of Analytical Options

A very interesting result gained through research of the relationship between retail and analytics is the breadth of the analytical activities actively used by retailers. Almost eighteen analytical trends have been highlighted  as ones that are frequently used by retailers for a wide range of purposes. On the other hand, there are some additional emerging analytical tools that should be adopted by those retailers who wish to gain a competitive edge over other tech-savvy retailers. Each of these tools provides immense value to the retail industry by tapping into its underlying potential.

However, due to the wide range of analytical tools available, it has become important for retail executives to fully understand which types of analytical activities actually match their organizational capabilities and strategies. Because they cannot pursue all the analytical possibilities at the same time or with equal rigor, they need to be able to target specific aspects of their business models and strategies with the help of analytics.

For instance, for certain companies, such as Nordstrom, Brooks Brothers, and Neiman Marcus, establishing a long-term relationship with their best customers is their ultimate goal. Each of these firms has developed a clienteling system that effectively captures customer interactions and manages the relationship between the company and the customers.

For such types of firms, integrating analytics into their clienteling systems assists them in fulfilling their objectives more effectively. Many years ago, Walmart had realised the importance of supply chain analytics in running the entire operations successfully while keeping the costs low and availability of products high.

RANDOM FACT
There are many kinds of analytical options available to retailers. Most use a combination of two or more tools to cover different areas of their businesses and to understand the needs and trends of customer behaviour in a greater detail.

It will not be ideal for a retailer that is focused on providing low-cost products or services to take his initial analytics efforts to address issues related to customer loyalty. The margins low-cost retailers achieve are unlikely to validate a premium for consumers for being loyal. Additionally, these retailers may not be in a position to afford the analytical and information infrastructure, including the technology and the people required to undertake a major analytical drive.

Instead of them focusing on customer loyalty, pricing and supply chain analytics will be more suited to such firms. Similarly, it will not be feasible for high-end retailers to equip only a few of their stores with site selection and supply chain analytics; they will be better off with analytical solutions to develop customer-oriented capabilities.

The particular influence of retailers should be based on their economic environments too. For instance, product selection, loyalty, and clienteling analytics are normally directed at increasing revenues during times of economic growth. In such challenging economic conditions, the retailers that are hard-pressed are more likely to go after analytical applications that focus on promotion effectiveness, price optimization, labour force analytics, and marketing mix allocation, each of these contributing to a reduction in cost while enhancing profitability quickly without too much investment.

Understanding the Prerequisites of Retail Analytics

Regardless of the type of analytical application or process, there are some important prerequisites of analytical progress in the retail industry that apply to almost every retail company.

Firstly, there is, of course, the data. No firm can do analytics without having high-quality, clean, accessible, and integrated data. It is fortunate that retailers now have many options that allow them to collect data, including from websites, point-of-sale transactions, loyalty programs, enterprise resource planning, and numerous analytical tools out there, such as Wi-Fi Shopper Intelligence Analytics.

RANDOM FACT
Tools like the Wi-Fi Shopper Intelligence Analytics provide an excellent way for brick-and-mortar stores to understand the behaviour of customers and help by providing crucial statistics that can be used to make smart business decisions to boost shoppers' experience at a store.

The data needs to be accessible and separated from transaction-oriented applications within which it was gathered. It should be in a place where analysts can easily access it to analyse it. Therefore, to cater this, many retailers provide access to such data through a data warehouse.

Many retail companies have single-purpose data marts and proliferated warehouses; however, because integration is crucial for advanced analytics, many of the most sophisticated retailers have their own enterprise data warehouse (EDW) from where they can easily draw crucial analytical applications.

Many retail executives and managers, when interviewed, have stated that their lives have become much easier as a result of implementing an EDW.

Another prerequisite of retail analytics is the interest, perhaps even passion, of the retail company's management in analytics. The success of any analytical application is highly dependent on the management's stance on it. Having a CEO who is really into the data or having a culture of making decisions based on facts can have a huge impact on the success and breadth of analytics in any company. It becomes natural to explore an increasing number of analytical processes with time. If, however, the management is not so keen, it will be a difficult battle for low-level analysts to get the necessary resources and the prioritization, especially in hard economic times.

A linked factor is the management team's desire and ability to develop their own analytics capabilities instead of relying on others to do so for them. Historically, the analysis work has mostly been done by manufacturers for those retailers who are in the business of packaged goods and grocery stores. However, the scene is changing with the introduction of sophisticated yet easy-to-use tools, such as Wi-Fi Analytics, that allow the retailers themselves to gather data and analyse it. These retailers are now beginning to manage their categories, optimise their shelf space, and monitor all their promotions and store traffic on their own.

Many retailers do not wish to share their analytical data with other manufacturers; therefore, the focus is now shifting with manufacturers offering solutions that provide the retailer a greater control over every facet of data collection and management.

Commonly Adopted Analytical Trends in the Retail Industry

This section will describe seven of the most common analytical trends that have been adopted by renowned retailers all over the world.

Shelf Space Allocation and Assortment Optimization

Type: Analytical process

Description: Shelf space and product inventory have always been very valuable resources for retailers. Analytics can now be used to effectively determine what types of products provide the greatest sales and highest profits. Shelf space allocations and assortments are being localised to store clusters or even at an individual-store level.

Optimization tools enable a retailer to perform analysis of each brand's profit contribution, pull-through analysis, together with the identification of any cannibalization effects.

Status: This analytical method quickly matures when it comes to microlevel analysis. At a macro level, it is utilised for store-specific or cluster-specific optimization. Initially, space optimization has been performed by manufacturers; however, it is evolving towards a joint process involving both key suppliers and retailers.

Customer-Driven Marketing

Type: Analytical process

Description: Ever since customers have become identifiable through credit or loyalty cards, retailers have taken strides in developing personalised offers and have modified their marketing approaches. These offers may be based on something as simple as extrapolations of existing consumer behaviour or may be something as complex as propensity models.

The offers may consist of products with a high chance of customer interest (i.e. next best offer), customised product displays, or targeted promotions.

Status: This method is mature yet continues to evolve for emerging technologies, such as mobile devices.

Fraud Detection and Prevention

Type: Analytical process

Description: Fraud detection is a major issue for those retailers who are determined to plug any losses and maintain consumer trust. Fraud can start off from a number of sources, including customers, individuals masquerading as the store's customers, store staff, or external elements, such as criminals or hackers.

Fraudulent merchandise returns and stolen credit card information are among the most recent frauds. Shrinkage, on the other hand, has been a long-term issue for those in the retail industry; however, certain analytical tools and approaches allow them to address such issues effectively.

Status: The problem of fraud is mature; however, the use of business intelligence and analytics for addressing fraud is relatively underpromising as criminals continue to improve their techniques.

Integrated Forecasting

Type: Analytical process

Description: Forecasting has been very important for retailers for a wide variety of functions. In many instances, different groups and functions develop their own sets of forecasts to inform staffing, ordering, budgeting, and merchandising. Some stores and regions develop bottom-up forecasts, while corporate develop top-down forecasts.

Now, a growing number of retailers are now centralizing their forecasting functions to develop integrated forecasts.

Status: Forecasting is extremely mature; however, it continues to evolve to become very sophisticated statistical forecasting technology.

Clustering and Localization

Type: Analytical process

Description: The period of standardization in retail is almost over. Retailers are now customizing—for the purpose of localization and various value proposition elements, such as pricing, assortments, store formats, staffing, and promotions.

Localization can be practiced on an individual-store level or, even more economically and commonly, to the store-cluster level.

Status: Clustering is quite mature. Level localization, on the other hand, is just emerging. It is less mature and is a trend that is common among a few hard goods and apparel retailers.

Marketing Mix Modelling

Type: Analytical process

Description: Marketing mix modelling assists retailers in determining the areas they should be spending their marketing resources on. They use econometric models to figure out whether or not a certain promotional approach, regardless of whether it is offline or online, will result in a considerable increase of sales.

Status: Marketing mix models are somewhat mature. The econometric tools have been on hand for several decades; however, the actual task of measuring the returns on the marketing mix models is very complex.

Pricing Optimization

Type: Analytical process

Description: After the turn of the millennium, retailers started to apply numerous revenue optimization models that were previously applied to airline seats and hotel rooms. In the retail industry, price optimization was first applied to the markdown pricing in apparel stores. Shortly after this, it was extended to the initial pricing and then to the everyday pricing at retail grocery.

Price optimization software requires point-of-sale information as the input, together with the seasonal sales data on an individual-store level. This data provides forecasting algorithms and data feeds probability to develop a set of demand curves for specific SKIs in certain stores or even clusters. This curve then positively identifies all products that are least and most price-sensitive.

Status: Markdown optimization is relatively mature among general merchandise and large apparel retailers. As for everyday price optimization, hard line and grocery chains are among the suitable candidates for this type of analytics.

CHAPTER 5: UNDERSTANDING WI-FI TRACKING

So far, we have learnt how important it is for retailers and businesses to understand the needs, wants, and behaviours of the consumers. We are also aware that online stores have multiple ways of gathering analytical data about their customers than the traditional brick-and-mortar stores. However, the scenario is changing, and changing fast.

According to a director of a think tank based in Washington, Jules Polonetsky,

The average wait time at the back register is two minutes. Half of your customers have been in your store twice in a week. Ten percent of the people who come in your store never come near a register, meaning they don't buy anything. There are a lot of people not finding what they want. The big promotion on the east side entrance of your store was more successful at bringing people to purchase than the promotion on the west side of your store. Here's the hotspot in your store that draws the most users. The typical user comes in and purchases one thing. Ten percent of your users have been at more than one of your stores. (Washington Post)

The listing of the insights is surprisingly accurate and specific. All this has been made possible through combining everyday technology and commercial ingenuity in a way they have never been intended to be used.

With the rapid increase in smartphones available in the market, the number of people using them has gone up at unprecedented rates. Every smartphone comes with a Wi-Fi card, and when this is on and searches for wireless networks to join, it can be detected by any routers in range. At home, the router connects to the smartphone, and you get access to the Internet. However, at a retail environment, there is equipment that can pick the signals sent out by your phone's Wi-Fi card and learn its unique ID, keeping track of the device's movement throughout the store. **This is what Wi-Fi tracking is all about: tracking the movement of customers in and around a retail store.**

Wi-Fi tracking has empowered retail brick-and-mortar stores to get precise data about the behaviour of their customers. It can be considered to be a physical version of the tools that online vendors have spent hundreds of thousands and millions of dollars in an attempt to perfect.

Hundreds and thousands of customer interactions each day are stored in logs and then uploaded to third-party company databases. These companies specialise in gathering and analysing analytical data.

How Wi-Fi Tracking Works

In order to distinguish themselves with other Bluetooth- or Wi-Fi-enabled devices, each smartphone/tablet comes with a unique MAC address. This twelve-digit code enables routers to send relevant data to the correct device. Note that MAC addresses have nothing to do with the electronics manufacturer Apple, even though all Apple devices that come with wireless technology also have a unique MAC address. By keeping a log of the MAC addresses of devices, retail stores can identify each device.

No personally identifiable data can be stored in this manner. However, just like it is with any form of metadata, the information collected through Wi-Fi tracking can be cross-referenced with other types of commercial or public information to build detailed consumer profiles; nonetheless, the identity of the consumers remains anonymous.

Privacy Matters

Even though the owner of the mobile device remains anonymous and only the movement is tracked to analyse the behaviour of the consumer, some people who are overly conscious about their privacy can be presented with an opt-out option that they can request the tracking service provider to NOT track them.

This option can be presented at the website of the Wi-Fi tracking firm, where users can enter the MAC addresses for each of the devices they own and have it removed from the list of devices tracked. Some retail analytics firms, however, do not provide this option.

In the near future, Bradish and the Wireless Registry and Future of Privacy Forum hope to develop a centralised Do Not Call list for MAC addresses. Theoretically, this will allow consumers to visit a specific website and register their devices' MAC address. From thereon, major tracking firms that have committed to this project will not track those devices as the consumers move around the brick-and-mortar stores.

This will be a type of self-regulation very similar to the way users now have immense control of their privacy over the Internet, where they can instruct web browsers to NOT allow websites to track them through cookies. Therefore, users always have an option to not be tracked regardless of whether it is an online store or a brick-and-mortar retail shop.

All in all, Wi-Fi tracking in physical stores is one among the most privacy-respecting ways of tracking consumers that do not collect any personal data at all.

The iConnect Shopper Intelligence Analytics: An Overview

Online stores have been leading the scene with their ability to collect, store, and then analyse customer metrics for quite some time now. The data collected can be used to derive effective marketing campaigns and promotions, besides other purposes.

Online retailers use various techniques to interact with their consumers to learn about their changing behaviour and shopping trends.

On the other hand, brick-and-mortar stores have generally been less fortunate than their Internet-based counterparts. To be able to overcome the challenges, brick-and-mortar retailers should develop an in-depth understanding of crucial data regarding the behaviour of walk-in customers, including things such as when the consumers visit the store, how they are engaged, and how frequently they return to the store.

iConnect is an IT solutions firm that specialises in providing tools and solutions that can help brick-and-mortar stores to better understand their customers. The iConnect *Shopper Intelligence Analytics, or SIA,* is a highly effective solution that uses two common technologies to achieve this—Wi-Fi and smartphones—in order to equip retailers with the ability to gather valuable insights throughout one or more of their stores.

How iConnect SIA Works

People use their mobile devices to search for and connect to Wi-Fi access points (AP). Even though not everyone has a smartphone or those that have one do not keep their Wi-Fi switched on all the time, statistics has shown that a relatively high number of people do keep their phone's Wi-Fi capability switched on when roaming in shopping centres and around shops, particularly because a growing number of stores now offer free Wi-Fi Internet access. These people can provide significant amounts of statistical data to allow retailers to learn their behaviour and changing shopping trends.

A few years back, physical stores were going through a period when they had lesser amount of sales and traffic data due to their inability to acquire expensive technologies such as laser traffic counters and video installations. These technologies were, however, impractical and inconvenient due to a number of reasons. For instance, they were not capable of generating the data that would reveal the crucial statistics related to customer engagement, the return visits, or the visits to various stores of the same retailer.

The iConnect SIA, a Wi-Fi tracking technology, has overcome these shortcomings and has solved the problem of collecting this critical data, which includes, but is not limited to, the following:
- ✓ The behaviour across locations
- ✓ The cross-location visits
- ✓ The behaviour of unique shoppers
- ✓ The duration of visits
- ✓ The number of return visits
- ✓ The number of unique shoppers

SIA provides retailers the ability to measure all the data and then analyse it to achieve a higher return on their investments. Apart from that, it also enables them to fully understand and identify the ongoing trends regarding their stores' performance.

Statistical Sampling

Statistical sampling is a very common and widely accepted business methodology used for collecting essential operational and marketing data. This method collects information based on the measurement and observation of a single or multiple factors throughout a specific group of population. The results are extrapolated in order to predict the major characteristics of the target population in general. This technique is fast and costs much less than if the entire target population is to be measured. Measuring the entire target population will be a very costly endeavour, not to mention impractical and time-consuming.

Due to these advantages, statistical sampling is widely used in a number of industries. Television ratings, for example, are an ideal example of statistical sampling in action. Nielsen Holdings, a global information and measurement company based in New York, gathers, collects, and reports the ratings and viewership in the TV industry all over the world. It achieves this by using complex sampling techniques.

The public health sector also uses statistical sampling to collect crucial data regarding the spread of illness and disease. For instance, the US Centers for Disease Control and Prevention develops the *Influenza Surveillance Report* on a weekly basis. The report includes data collected through the process of statistical sampling in all the fifty

A graphical view of the data collected by the Centers for Disease Control and Prevention (Source: CDC)

state health departments as well as 120 laboratories and two thousand healthcare institutes across one hundred cities all over the US. This data is then depicted in a graphical form, as shown on the right.

It is crucial to ensure accuracy and reliability of the statistics that the data is collected from a large segment of the target population.

Over 50 per cent of the population in developed countries own a smartphone. Therefore, these mobile devices are ideal in gathering statistical samples for analytical purposes as well as for predicting consumer behaviour in stores, malls, coffee shops, and numerous other public places.

An example of data collection through statistical sampling (Source: Nielsen)

Consumers and the Use of Mobile Devices

It is important to discuss and reveal some studies that shed light on how dependent consumers are on their smartphones while shopping.

A study was carried out by IBM[4] in 2012 in which it surveyed shoppers across eight developed nations. The study found that over 45 per cent of the shoppers owned and used at least two or more types of technologies when shopping at brick-and-mortar stores. The technologies used were usually a combination of a PC-based search on the Internet and a smartphone.

---

4 *'Capitalising on the Smarter Consumer'*, IBM, SOURCE.

The capabilities of a mobile device cannot be undermined when it comes to enhancing the shopping experience of a consumer. According to consumers themselves, as revealed by a research, it was found that the top four uses of a mobile device for a consumer before they purchased something were to

1. **find the location of a store,**
2. **check prices,**
3. **carry out research on an item, and**
4. **read purchase reviews.**

These four points do not only apply when they are in their homes or at their offices but also when they are in the close vicinity of a mall, a store, or a coffee shop where there is Wi-Fi access available. The renowned Nielsen study *Mobile Devices Empower Today's Shoppers In-Store and Online*[5] indicated that almost 78 per cent of shoppers agreed to the fact that they used their smartphones to locate a store, while around 63 per cent confirmed that they checked prices of items online before buying them at a brick-and-mortar store.

Shopping Trends and Retailers

The trend of using smartphones while shopping has very important implications for the retailers. Unfortunately, many retailers do not understand how to take advantage of this opportunity.

Up till now, any wireless applications for retail have simply been limited to technologies the like of barcode scanners, which have only helped reach a higher level of efficiency in supply chain and overall operations. Nevertheless, as mobile devices continue to transform the lifestyle of consumers, the retailers must also adapt and develop a mindset that helps them appreciate the altered nature of shopping.

In a recent study, retailers were asked about their views on incorporating mobility, and 47 per cent of them believed that the whole idea of their mobile strategy was only to improve their brand. Not only that, but another 45 per cent went on to disclose that mobility was indeed an effective way to enhance the outreach of their online offerings. However, when they were questioned about what kind of investments they had made to enhance the experience of their customers who visit their brick-and-mortar stores, it was surprising to see that not many had taken action in this regard.

This gap between technology utilization has put the consumers in the front seat after raising their expectations to new levels, thereby creating more challenges for the retailers.

The solution is simple. Retailers should invest in technologies like iConnect Shopper Intelligence Analytics, using which can help them gather a deeper insight into the habits and behaviour of their customers. This valuable data can then be used to drive sales and enhance the overall customer experience.

SIA: Use of Wi-Fi Signals

The smartphones that have their Wi-Fi capability switched ON are connected to a Wi-Fi network or are trying to find a network to connect to emit certain 'Wi-Fi messages'. The frequency at which they transmit these messages varies, depending on whether they are trying to connect to a Wi-Fi access point (AP) or whether they are already connected and transmitting data. The frequency is also dependent on the manufacturer of the mobile device as well as the status of the device. In general, most phones send out messages anywhere between two and nine times a minute.

---

5 *'Mobile Devices Empower Today's Shoppers In-Store and Online', Nielsen, SOURCE.*

The following table will give you a relatively accurate figure in different circumstances:

Connected to an AP	Location-Based Services On	Average Wi-Fi Requests per Minute
No	No	2
No	Yes	2
Yes	No	5
Yes	Yes	9

Each message sent out by the smartphone (or any other mobile device, such as a tablet) consists of two standard headers, which are as follows:

1. The RADIO HEADER
2. The 802.11 HEADER

The *radio header* contains all the information related to the characteristics of the message, such as the strength of the signal, the time stamp, and the channel information.

The *802.11 header*, on the other hand, contains the 802.11 frame, including its source, packet type, and destination.

The iConnect SIA proprietary technology is capable of automatically and passively detecting the location of shoppers as well as staffers by sensing the Wi-Fi probe messages from their smartphones.

It is precisely this information that is necessary for successfully charting the purchasing habits and behaviours of customers.

Classification of Data

The SIA uses a number of criteria to classify all the devices that come within the range of its sensors. This is important because signal strength, when considered alone, is not a very reliable method of classifying devices as it's highly inaccurate. This is mainly because Wi-Fi signals tend to weaken as a result of attenuation as well as multipath in indoor environments. To add to that, the strength of the signal also depends on several real-time conditions, including the number of people present inside a store or any changes to the floor set/furniture in close proximity to the access point.

The following graph reveals that the signal threshold of the number of visitors inside the store changes with time.

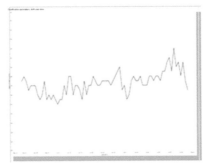

Changes over time: classification parameters

The accuracy can be increased by adding duration time thresholds, which are based on the idea that visitors tend to stay for an extended period of time in the store than has been previously assumed.

In order to further enhance classifications and cater to the environmental factors, SIA's algorithms use unsupervised machine-learning techniques to regulate the signal in real time, as well as the duration thresholds.

The unsupervised learning tends to add a feedback loop to the data classification process in order to compare the patterns of numerous parameters, including the number of devices detected, the strength of the signal, and the duration over time with the patterns that were recorded in the same shop or store.

Additionally, the SIA also compares the recorded patterns with similar stores that are present on the iConnect Network. Time windows and unique thresholding values can be developed through this calibration process, thus refining the data accuracy and quality with time.

The iConnect SIA also features a supervised learning technique that incorporates another feedback loop to the data classification process. With this, iConnect SIA has the ability to insert truth data into the process in order to enhance the accuracy and quality of analytics. This added feedback may be as easy as adding the timings of the store to being as sophisticated as adding information such as transactional or staffing data or integrating customers' traffic.

Truth data reduces undersampling and oversampling in environments that have heavy traffic, including any busy neighbouring shops.

The consequences of undersampling and oversampling can be understood by reviewing the following charts:

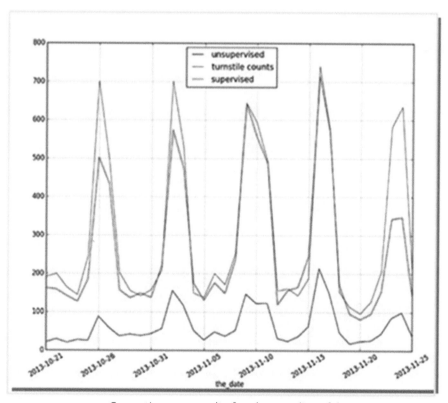

Correction as a result of undersampling of data

39

SIA is also capable of correcting the data classification in order to prevent rapid growth of smartphone adoption from biased visit counts. A necessary level of granularity is not provided by third-party estimates of the penetration of smartphones; this is exactly why SIA applies the regional benchmark data inside its own network to adjust guest counts. For instance, if the unadjusted visit count reaches 35.5 per cent over a year, this figure will not link with customer sales transaction data. As can be seen in the following graphs, SIA has the ability to cater for the increase in smartphone penetration results to get a more realistic and accurate year-by-year increase of visit rates amounting to 5.5 per cent.

SIA and Privacy

Customers are more concerned about their privacy now than they have ever been; this is why iConnect SIA has dedicated to address the privacy concerns of both retailers and consumers.

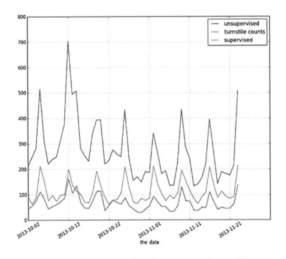

Correction as a result of oversampling of data

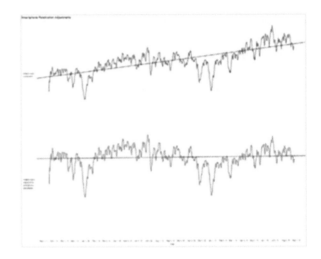

Adjustment of smartphone penetration

The reports provided to retailers do not contain any personal information of the customers at all. No attempt is made to link the data collected—behavioural or otherwise—to any of the customers.

The sensors used by SIA simply do not collect any personally identifiable information that can identify who the customers are, who they call upon, or what kind of websites they visit. The only information that is collected is the one that is broadcasted by Wi-Fi smartphones and Wi-Fi access points to which the consumers connect. This information includes the following:
1. Station ID—the MAC address of the device that is transmitting
2. BSSID ID—the MAC address of the access point to which the device is connected
3. Signal strength of the device that is transmitting
4. Transmission time stamp
5. The frequency or channel of transmission

The privacy of individual customers is ensured by anonymization of all recorded MAC addresses of the smartphones that were within the range of retailer Wi-Fi access points. This is achieved by the use of a nonreversible hashing algorithm on each of the MAC addresses. This method generates a new ID, which can never be linked again with the same smartphone.

The process of hashing algorithm is performed in two distinct stages:

1. A reliable and renowned one-way cryptographic MD5 algorithm is used to create a message digest of 128-bit strength. The MAC address (48-bit) is hashed with a 64-bit secret key, thus creating the 128-bit message digest.

2. To further disguise the hash and to induce a theoretical data loss, the second stage of this algorithm is used to compress the 128-bit message digest into an identifier (64-bit).
   This results in an identifier that is safely stored on SIA cloud and cannot be reverse-engineered to produce the original MAC address.

Additionally, it is recommended that retailers disclose to shoppers about the ongoing foot traffic analysis. Guidelines can be provided by iConnect to help retailers create notices that can be posted onto visible locations to inform the customers. As a result of these notices, customers who do not wish to participate can easily opt out of the analysis.

CHAPTER 6: WHEN BIG DATA MEETS BUSINESS ANALYTICS

Imagine if you can harness the power of information in order to develop a demand-driven supply chain and merchandising, reduce costs, and drive your operations to new heights in an attempt to deliver an amazing shopping experience that leaves your competitors way behind.

Business analytics makes all this possible.

In today's fast-paced age of information, it has become extremely important to not only manage but properly understand data. Retail constantly generates a lot of data (such as transaction logs), but now, as big data enters the scene, there is much more to look at!

There has been an implosion of business and customer data in various forms, and this has created huge challenges for the retailers. Consumers are now more connected, more demanding, and more empowered, and they are able to choose how, where, and when they want to make purchases.

Retail organizations with a forward-looking approach are armed with such data and know how to translate it into actionable insights. These retailers are turning the challenges into a number of profitable opportunities while continuing to build customer loyalty. The transformation in the way of thinking and the approach of retailers has empowered retailers to not only understand the history but also analyse what's currently ongoing in the market in order to be able to predict future trends.

This chapter focuses on how you can harness the data in order to successfully identify pain points, which may be having an adverse effect on your growth. You will also learn how you can extract important information to soothe such 'pains'.

Harnessing the Data: Volume, Variety, Veracity, and Velocity

As has been mentioned earlier, data is being collected at unprecedented rates. Retailers are now increasingly working to gather, organise, and use the data to gain insights that drive decisions and actions to achieve enhanced customer loyalty and satisfaction. The ultimate aim is to increase bottom line profits. Business analytics makes data capture, its translation, and the next action possible.

RANDOM FACT

Consumers always leave behind clues and signals regarding their needs, wants, and expectations.

It takes skill and the right technology to decipher this data and use it to your advantage.

Retail stores are increasingly employing technologies to gather this data and use it to better understand their customers.

Today, virtually everything has been digitalised, and this creates new types of real-time data across numerous industries, including retail. As we are writing this book, almost 2.5 quintillion bytes of data are being created all over the world, with around 17 terabytes coming from Twitter and Facebook alone. Consider this: 90 per cent of this data currently in this world has been created in the last two years; additionally, there are no signs of any stopping or slowing of the rate at which data is created. As a matter of fact, the speed and volume at which this data is created will surely bring around new challenges to the retailers in the coming years.

To make things more challenging and difficult, most of the data is in unstructured and nontraditional forms. Firms struggle to ascertain the accuracy of most of this data; therefore, they need to measure and combine the data across numerous sources in order to be sure of the accuracy and usefulness of the information.

These facts are igniting questions as to what the best way to capture such data will be and how the insights should be derived from the data that has an impact on the retailer's strategy. For many retailers, the answer lies in tapping into the advantages of various advanced analytics technologies as well as strategies. These insights can help them retain their existing pool of customers while attracting new ones. One such technology that we have discussed in the previous chapter is the Wi-Fi tracking technology used to track and gather data regarding the actual movement of customers at a physical store.

The analytics helps create various opportunities for the retailers to meet the demands of their customers and gain a competitive advantage over others in the marketplace.

Recognizing the Pain Points of Retail

Before you are able to properly harness the power of data, you need to first understand what problems you want the data to solve for you. For many retailers, the challenges are related to providing an omnichannel shopping experience for the consumers in the most efficient way possible. This experience will allow today's consumers to interact with a business online, over the phone, using a mobile device, from a catalogue, at a kiosk, and of course, in a physical store.

With you as a retailer, your goal should be to provide the correct type of product at the ideal price, at the right place, and that too, at the correct time. There are, however, many obstacles that you will have to face on the way to success.

When you begin to get deeply involved in this challenge, you will have to identify what your customers want and then work on the dynamics of supply and demand in order to deliver that to them based on their expectations.

In the end, you will need the best tools if you want to win over customers and create brand loyalty while avoiding unnecessary expenses.

Asking the Crucial Questions

Retailers are taking certain steps to enhance their efficiency, improve the level of experience they offer their customers, and develop intelligent retailing strategies every day. This is a race, and the retailers who do not try to win it will be left far behind.

To figure out whether or not your organization or store is working intelligently in retail, answer the following crucial questions:
- To what level does your staff have access to information that they need at the place and time they need it?
- With which suppliers do you have to move to constructive collaboration from just cooperation?
- Which of your organization's operational processes are capable of adapting and responding swiftly to the rapidly changing demands of the market?
- What amount of value are you gaining from the information stored at your company? How much of the external information do you use within your strategy as well as decision-making processes?
- How well aware are you of your consumers' preferences?

Extracting Meaning from the Gigantic Amounts of Data

Data comes in from a number of sources, channels, systems, and regions through the day and night. The ultimate challenge is how this data should be consolidated and organised and have its meaning extracted to make informed decisions that enhance productivity and agility.

The keys that are needed to unlock the hidden mysteries of this data are embedded in business analytics. The business analytics tools of today offer utmost flexibility, user-friendly reporting, modelling, analysis, as well as predictive and planning capability to make it easy for everyone in your organization to access the data they need to make educated decisions across all locations, departments, roles, and functions.

An Interconnected Firm

Regardless of whether you have a single store at a single location or multiple stores spread across the entire nation, it is crucial for you to develop an interconnected company where every employee has access to the crucial data they need to perform their roles and duties as efficiently as possible.

Do not forget that industry leaders are renowned by their ability to use all the information, all the perspective, all the people, and all the decisions at the exact point of impact. The insight-driven retailer has the chance to enhance the performance in many critical areas of an organization (and your store) by doing the following:
- Creating and developing a smarter and efficient shopping experience imply that a particular retailer uses the insight into customer behaviour and their purchasing patterns in order to provide a very

personalised path to buying a product or service. This, in turn, increases brand loyalty and customer advocacy.

- Developing smarter merchandising as well as supply networks allows a retailer to provide the right products and services to the customers at the right place and at the right time at the right cost. This increases the revenue while minimizing markdowns and stock-outs, and of course, it protects the margin.
- Driving smart operations, the retailer improves planning and becomes more agile in the retail environment. It keeps its stores, assets, labour, and all business processes aligned with its strategic initiatives and corporate KPIs (key performance indicators). KPIs are the specifications used to track business objectives. This also creates a healthy environment, comprising accountability, visibility, and collaboration.

The Pillars of Business Analytics

Business analytics consists of a wide range of technologies, strategies, and practices that are used to comprehend and improve the performance of a business. Read on to learn more about the pillars of business analytics.

Business Intelligence (BI)

Business intelligence (BI) comprises of methods, concepts, and numerous technologies that are used to gather and study the data in order to drive improved decision-making processes.

BI was introduced around 1958, when Hans Peter Luhn, an IBM researcher, first utilised the term. A couple of decades later, numerous technologies have surfaced that have transformed BI into a function of mainstream business.

> **RANDOM FACT**
> The pillars of business analytics include the following:
> ✔ Business intelligence (BI)
> ✔ Advanced analytics (AA)
> ✔ Performance management (PM)

BI utilises reporting, querying, scorecards, analysis, and dashboards to simplify things for businesses throughout the organization in their attempt to find, study, and share useful information that is needed to enhance decision-making.

Ad hoc functionality, drill down, mobility, visualization, and drill through are a few of BI's capabilities that enable users to comprehend the prevailing state of a business, including why the business is operating at that level.

While BI has improved significantly over the years, its capabilities continue to increase and evolve as they provide deeper insights, which can be applied throughout the organization by any concerned user. Without this type of evolution, companies will not be able to flourish in the fast-paced business world of today, where big data is of a paramount importance.

Advanced Analytics (AA)

Advanced analytics (AA) takes advantage of the historical, the current, and the future possibilities to assist retailers in viewing potential results if they make and execute specific decisions. AA comprises of predictive modelling, statistics, data mining, what-if simulation, and text analytics to positively identify the patterns and any correlations in sets of data to predict events in the future. It also provides an assessment of the attractiveness of varying courses of action.

The algorithms are capable of automatically finding significant patterns, and the models continuously learn from the past data and update the predictions for new and current business questions.

With the help of AA, retailers can move from traditional foundational reporting to breakaway and differentiating capabilities, which ultimately gives them a competitive advantage. AA also enables the retailer to effectively predict a customer's response to a specific offer and allows them to use the result to draw any conclusions regarding their supply chain requirements, financial performance, and operational needs.

For retail organizations, AA is no less than a game changer as it allows them to generate greater results and improves their efficiency with better insights and information into the predictions of future outcomes.

Performance Management (PM)

Performance management (PM) allows for a structured, simplified, automated, and dynamic modelling in order to understand the repercussions of numerous scenarios. BI, along with AI, drives the entire input to the what-if planning in performance management.

PM gives businesses immense flexibility to create best-case and worst-case scenarios. For instance, modelling the outcomes of the changes in demand of a product and then pushing the scenario through to operations and merchandising can give a retailer a clear picture of its impact. Eventually, it drives those decisions to finance and allows the organization to comprehend its effects on the company's bottom line.

PM also creates an opportunity to link operational and financial plans through rolling forecasts and driver-based modelling and provides users the access and visibility to the correct information at the ideal time, which builds confidence in the data and its results.

The modelling environment also makes sure that there is consistency between the strategy and the field execution while creating a culture of constant planning. It keeps the company aligned to its strategic objectives.

Risk management is an additional string accompanying performance management. It helps the company (or a retailer) understand and act in accord with the numerous risk areas—including credit, market, and liquidity risks—to solidify decisions while satisfying the internal and external requirements for governance.

Analytical Decision Management: The Advantage

As far as retail is concerned, the decision-making processes are rarely automated in most of the organizations. Majority of managers spend precious hours one after the other to collect data, crunch numbers, and perform collective checks in meetings. Sadly, these old methods do not always result in market success.

In today's competitive global marketplace, the competitive advantage lies in managing, optimizing, and automating decisions through a solution called *Analytical Decision Management (ADM)*. ADM allows managers to effectively prioritise and implement strategies quicker than their competitors can in the marketplace through informed choices.

> ### RANDOM FACT
> A business has to make three types of decisions to successfully cater to the changing demands of consumers and fluctuating conditions of the market. These are
> 1. strategic decisions,
> 2. tactical decisions, and
> 3. operational decisions.

As an entrepreneur, a store manager, or a key decision maker within your organization, your challenge is to utilise all data during the decision-making process while knowing that there is a huge amount of data with lesser amount of time to thoroughly analyse in order to make informed choices. ADM comes in to help and guide you to make the business processes smoother as well as the customer interactions better. It does so even when conditions are changing by implementing business rules and a thorough decision-making process framework and, through predictive analytics, by effectively optimizing and automating decisions, enhancing outcomes, and successfully solving certain business problems.

Making Risk-Aware and Informed Decisions

The ultimate goal is to optimise the decision-making process to lead to improved business results. However, it is also crucial to understand the kinds of decisions that need to be made, who has ownership of the decisions, and whether or not the decisions will have the ability to get the right data and understanding of all the information that is critical to the organization's success.

Risk management solutions assist retail organizations in making risk-aware decisions through risk management methodologies and programs. The end result is an **enhanced business performance and increased bottom line**.

A potential for risk management can assist your business in achieving a steady growth and can help it address the ever-increasing demands for compliance with regulations in today's complex and volatile markets. To be more exact, risk management solutions help companies by
  ✓ enhancing their decision-making by offering insight, risk analysis, and optimum transparency;
  ✓ enhancing the return on capital by taking risk-informed decisions that can help companies and their managers to fully optimise the allocation of capital;
  ✓ speeding up the streamlining of the risk processes in order to bring down the loss from credit losses, all this by managing the operational risk;
  ✓ reducing the expenses associated with regulatory compliance; and
  ✓ dynamically evolving with the organization's risk architecture to effectively adopt as regulations, market demands, and risk management practices change.
Generally speaking, there are three types of decisions: tactical, strategic, and operational. There is, however, some amount of crossover between each of these types.

When a manager or business owner is equipped with a clean knowledge of these types of decisions, he or she can determine which ones can be automated and duly optimised for the benefit of the retail business. *Here, the key to success is in optimizing and automating the decisions in specific ways—ways that make the data-driven strategy the basis of any action.*

Setting Direction through Strategic Decisions

There is no denying the fact that strategic decisions establish the long-term direction for a company regardless of what industry it operates in. A strategic decision can be the base from which certain tactical decisions can be made. You need to understand that strategic decisions require immense flexibility and are regularly made as a comeback to, or in, the expectation of changes in market conditions.

It is clear that online stores are continuing to transform the entire retail and consumer markets. This is why it is crucial to understand the decision-making processes and not only reduce risk but also lead a retail store to fight back and retain its former glory.

Getting back to the topic of strategic decision-making, those who are involved in making these types of decisions are normally executives (C-level), directors, and vice presidents. These individuals make the decisions such as which level of consumer segments has to be targeted, which channels the company should invest in, and whether or not they need to acquire another company to expand their own market coverage.

By utilizing business analytics, these decision makers can assess the scenarios and explore possible outcomes before they actually make any moves.

Getting the Visibility to Make Tactical Decisions

Tactical decisions typically require forming of policies and/or processes while focusing on a certain objective or project that has been executed at the operational level. They provide a business the ability to make their operational decisions more anticipatory and similar, and they are propelled by the need to establish repeatable, scalable, and efficient processes through the use of accurate and timely data.

Tactical decisions need visibility into a business and an in-depth understanding of the external conditions and the influences as well as decision makers, including system managers, business managers, and business analytics, who are responsible for making the decisions regarding numerous issues, such as the category mix and returns policies and the promotions guidelines.

Making Operational Decisions by Leveraging Real-Time Information

Operational decisions are the front-line actions that normally implement a process, policy, or set of rules for a specific case. These decisions make the outcomes more predictable and consistent. Accurate, real-time information is needed when making operational decisions for optimal effectiveness. Keeping in mind the fast-paced environment that surrounds operational decisions, it is crucial to provide the information in a format that is easy to consume and is in a format specific to its role.

The following individuals are the operational decision makers:
- ✓ Customer service representatives
- ✓ Store managers
- ✓ Sales associates
- ✓ Marketing managers
- ✓ Automated systems (e.g. website recommendation engines)

The individuals in any of the above roles make crucial decisions regarding problems, such as when the company should try to upsell a customer or when a refund issue should be addressed or what products should be put offered on a promotion.

Aligning the Outcomes to the Business Strategy

Business analytics technologies that are available today are friendly enough to allow any contributor in a company to derive useful insights, and that too with a minimal learning curve.

Even though the short-term return on investment on various business analytics tools can be huge (even when they are deployed in remote areas), you need to make sure that you buy in from your company's stakeholders in order to get the most value out of these tools. In addition to that, it will also transform your organization/store into one that is integrated with visibility and transparency into data.

The importance of making a case for business analytics with the business users, executives, and numerous other stakeholders cannot be undermined. This is because all decision makers in your

> **RANDOM FACT**
> For data to be beneficial, its real value needs to be extracted. Using business analytics tools, retailers can overcome these challenges surrounding data and can put it to practical use for their advantage.

organization need to fully support the company's efforts to implement technology and practices if they are to unleash the true potential and drive maximum positive impact on sales and profits.

Recently, an IBM CEO study[6] was conducted, in which the participants were questioned how effective their companies were in drawing value from the gathered data. Access, insights, and action were the three dimensions across which the companies were capable of leveraging data in order to make certain decisions. These companies were recognised as outperformers and effectively surpassed their peers. They were insight driven and only used the insights to make crucial business decisions.

The Value of Analytics

Data on its own is of no use at all. As a matter of fact, unless real value is extracted from it, the data can be tremendously overwhelming. Business analytics can assist retailers to effectively overcome four challenges surrounding data:

1. **Inability to act as one**
   Planning capabilities allow sharing of decisions, the impact to be fully understood, the issues to be negated, and the strategies to be duly implemented at front line.
2. **Lack of insight**
   Retailers need to have the strategic insight into an organization's performance in order to prevent managers from making any critical decisions without crucial information.
3. **Inability to predict**
   Predictive capabilities result in better decision-making. Without decision makers having advanced modelling capabilities and a clear understanding of the real factors that drive performance, some decisions that turn out to be quite costly for the organization may be made.
4. **Inefficient access**
   Many of the managers do not have access to crucial information that they need in order to perform their jobs effectively. Without having this, they are often forced to make decisions based on their instincts instead of insight.

Aligning around the Impact Point

The whole of retail organization is affected, and it has to be aligned around the impact point, ranging from merchandising to operations to marketing to human resources and beyond. Business analytics can help businesses do the following:

- ✓ Give their merchandising team the capacity to change and adjust assortments based on the insight into customer purchasing patterns as well as location, demographic, and other factors that drive demand.
- ✓ Make human resources secure the correct resources and create staffing as well as hiring plans, depending on the growth forecasts and required skill sets. It can also get it to develop compensation targets and plans that have been aligned with the corporate strategy as well as customer loyalty.
- ✓ Improve operational efficiencies by enhancing and optimizing the inventory while minimizing markdowns and stock-outs. This will result in increased revenues and stronger margins.
- ✓ Enable marketers to utilise consumer data from varying sources and allow them to develop granular and relevant customer segments. They can also personalise promotions to encourage and motivate consumers to make a purchase.
- ✓ Align the corporate goals and the key performance indicators (KPIs) around the company's strategy. This will reduce operating costs and enhance profitability, not to mention align the finance to the company's operations.
- ✓ Integrate budgets, plans, and forecasts across distribution, merchandising, stores, and finance to

---

6 *'IBM Global CEO Study', IBM, SOURCE.*

develop efficiencies, diminish bottlenecks, and increase profits.

✓ Develop a unique brand experience and build stronger customer loyalty regardless of the channel used by providing the customer-facing staff access to crucial information that they need to comprehend consumer reactions, preferences, and experiences. It also empowers the employees to integrate the insights for execution at numerous digital channels, including mobile, e-commerce, kiosks, and others.

✓ Assist store managers in increasing same-store sales using predictions and forecasts and empower the store managers to review the insight into consumer data, impact of promotions, assortment plans and enable them to manage the controllable expenses for optimization of their profit and loss (P&L).

Business analytics tools can enhance the performance as well as the results in almost every retail organization while keeping its functions centred on the corporate strategy and the company's success.

CHAPTER 7: MARKETING IN THE CUSTOMER-DRIVEN ERA

Retail has undergone a significant transformation, and wise retailers are always trying to work on refining the experience of their customers in an attempt to retain their current customers while trying to get new ones. The reason retail has not changed is only because of factors such as advancements in technology and globalization. The retail industry has transformed as a result of the changes among the consumers themselves.

These two realities, when combined, pose a serious challenge as well as opportunities for the retailers of today.

Beyond technology, economic conditions, and the shifting competition, there are two most powerful influences on the retailers, which include the rise in the social media and the increasing number of channels available through which purchases can be made. It should be pointed out that the rise in digital media has had a huge impact on consumer behaviour.

This has led retail marketers to change and adjust their current approach of marketing strategies from one that is product driven to one that is consumer driven. In actuality, retailers have to continuously strive to not only meet but also exceed the expectations of their customers when delivering a shopping experience. The only way in which it is possible for retailers to succeed is through the use of crucial business analytics, which can help them gain actionable insights, with the ultimate focus on developing customer loyalty.

Getting to Know the Consumer Behaviour and Trends

An increasing number of retailers are now leveraging critical consumer data, both within and outside their organization, in an attempt to attract, retain, and grow the number of their customers. By understanding their consumers, their influencers, their affinities, how they prefer to buy things, and to which offers they are likely to respond, retailers can get a better understanding of the target audience. This information helps retailers provide better service to their customers, making the right kinds of offers at the ideal time.

> **RANDOM FACT**
> *Customer behaviour* refers to the study of groups, organizations, or individuals as well as the processes they use to secure, select, use, or dispose of products, services, and experiences and the impacts these processes have on the customers and the society.

It also assists retailers in uncovering the upsell and the cross-sell opportunities, hence maximizing marketing dollars. When your business is able to deliver targeted offers that are valued by customers, you can avoid all the unnecessary promotional expenses or even discounting. Similarly, product markdowns can take place even before the product loses its level of attraction, hence generating certain profit. The resources can also be reassigned to focus on the most profitable areas.

To be able to leverage data for the purpose of insights, it is very important to keep in mind the five *C*s of the path that customers take to purchase something. These five *C*s are
1. customer,
2. context,
3. community,
4. content, and
5. commerce.

We will now briefly discuss each of the *C*s mentioned above.

Utilizing *Customer* Data

Customer data is one of the most crucial forms of data for a particular retailer. It is important for retailers to properly organise and use customer data if they are to benefit from it. Many retailers are now moving towards advanced customer segmentation, from the segments of many to the segments of only a few to the segments of one. This is based on a deep understanding of what the customer data portrays.

Keep in mind that this information regarding the customer can come from many number and types of sources. This is precisely why when the data is consolidated, the real insights tend to be generated. Using this insight, retailers are able to analyse the preferences and purchase patterns of each segment, determine the actions that may encourage a consumer or consumers to take action to the correct offer, and use techniques such as advanced modelling in order to predict their chances of responding to a potential offer.

Putting Data in *Context*

After the retailer has understood the buying patterns and preferences of consumers, he or she can use the customer data in terms for a broader context. For instance, you have the option of combining external data, such as demographic details and weather patterns, to examine performance drivers. You may even join it with internal data, such as the stock level of the items that a client is interested in.

Context refers to a situation in which your consumers may end up. It may be about the delivery of a real-time proposition that records the device they use, the time of the day, and how they manage to visit a certain website.

This portrays the concept that numerous people have varying levels of preferences and behaviours, depending on what they do and where they are. For instance, on Monday morning, they may be using their tablets or iPads when commuting, or they may be using computers on weekends. Visiting a store or talking directly to sales personnel must also be accounted for.

It must be kept in mind that not all customers will respond to similar products in the same way, even with the same type of offer. They will also not respond in a similar manner at other instances; therefore, it is important to provide context to the data to help you make perceptive decisions about what you should offer to the customer.

Connecting with the Consumer *Communities*

Apart from the information that you possess about the consumers through interactions, there are many other influencers that greatly impact a customer's decision to move towards making a purchase. If the retailer spends time to understand the consumer's sentiments, the communities, and other influencers along with information about how their retail brands are perceived through these various channels, the right decisions can be made, and highly effective targeted offers can be made to the consumer.

By taking advantage of influencer comments and ratings, you will be able to make your offers stronger and more competent.

Keeping the *Content* in Mind

Besides having a great deal of information about the customer and their community and other influencers, internal content also plays a crucial role in driving a particular offer and in encouraging a customer to buy a product or service.

> **RANDOM FACT**
> The five **C**s describe the path that a customer takes to buy a product. Retailers must focus on the five **C**s to streamline the buying process for their potential customers.

A retailer has to ensure that the right kinds of products are available through the right types of channels. This means that a retailer needs to integrate marketing, merchandising, and supply chain to the path to purchase that is created for the consumer. In addition, certain promotions can be driven based on the current stock levels, thereby creating opportunities that can effectively shift the slow-moving products/services and enhance profit margins.

Getting to the Personalised *Commerce* Part

A personalised approach is favoured by consumers when it comes to their shopping experience, regardless of the preferred method of commerce or touchpoint. Retailers are continuing to refine the road to personalization in order to retain their current customers and grow their customer base to generate more profit.

Analysing Unstructured Data

If you are a successful retail leader, you will probably be on the lookout for new business insights to propel your business forwards. Your way of working will involve identifying the root cause of the problems, spotting opportunities rapidly, and then anticipating and exploiting the future trends of the market. To achieve all this, you will have turned your attention to business intelligence solutions in order to track the key metrics related to your business and the consumers. Business intelligence involves concepts, technologies, and methods that collect, analyse, and put forth data to allow enhanced decision-making.

However, this isn't the entire picture. Throughout an enterprise and on the Internet, the market addresses volumes. Prospects, customers, and influencers fill out forms, write comments, and talk to marketing, sales, and customer service staff. Prior to making any decisions, all this information should be taken into account. Anecdotal and instinct information can also greatly contribute to sane decision-making. However, this is unstructured data and is much different from what businesses normally analyse in business intelligence. So what should be done with unstructured content? Find out in the next section.

The Challenge of Unstructured Data

The volume of unstructured content is so expansive that almost 80 per cent of all the information generated and collected on a daily basis is unstructured. Some portions of this data are held internally, whereas a major portion of this unstructured content is found on the Internet, in the form of tweets, blogs, and online interactions and exchanges between a consumer and a customer support/service staff.

The data contains some of the most valuable and relevant business information. This free-form or semistructured information is often prone to escaping careful inspection.

Because of the fact that it is not organised, it becomes much more difficult to take advantage of. The information cannot be queried like a simple database even though it contains crucial business information, which can be utilised to identify the preferences of customers, support concerns, competitor position, product quality, supplier feedback, and various other critical information that can help you as a retailer.

Identifying the Opportunities Presented by Untapped Analytics

Wise retailers understand the importance of reviewing this untapped analytics. For instance, many companies may use this data to answer the following questions:
- Do the consumers communicate our brand?
- What do the customers say about the new format of our new store?
- Do customers recommend our products and services to their family and friends?
- What unmet demands are emerging?

Retailers and retail companies need to have a highly systematic method of finding, distilling, and analysing the huge amounts of unstructured data in existence today.

There are numerous analytics solutions that can provide the answer. Content analytics, together with social media analytics, is becoming common within business analytics in empowering organizations to effectively unlock the crucial insights found within the unstructured content, regardless of whether it is held externally or internally.

Decision-Making Driven by Customers

It is a growing practice where retail managers supplement the insights from business intelligence reports with the anecdotal data regarding variables of the external market. They do this by reading blog pages, analysing product reviews, and engaging with customers and the field employees of the organization. Not accounting for the efficiency of this approach, the fact that this method is subjective and time-consuming cannot be denied.

Since the advent of social media and content analytics, retail organizations have gained a powerful and objective method of gathering business insights from the huge quantities of unstructured data. This enables them to shift from data-driven decision-making processes to those that are customer driven. The latter takes into account both the external and internal variables to ensure most favourable decision-making.

For a moment, let's discuss the example of a certain retail chain that is required to make a decision regarding whether or not it should invest into a new, private-label product line.

The retailer, using data-driven evidence, seems to have reliable information regarding the costs as well as the sales trends linked with this particular product line.

By adding insights from the external market, the retailer can enjoy a more detailed overview of the entire marketplace, including the perceptions and preferences of the customers and the competitors.

By combining these two data streams, the management of the retail company is more capable of making the correct decision regarding the feasibility of launching a new product line.

Content Analytics

Those retailers who make use of content analytics to observe and act on specifically targeted areas—such as warranty issues, customer complaints, and fraudulent claims—can greatly enhance their return on investment (ROI) while having a positive impact on their bottom line. In this section, you will learn about content analytics and observe it in action.

This is an example of a renowned language lessons retailer that wanted to capture and review the consumer responses in an attempt to reveal trends hidden within the text. To achieve this, the retailer turned towards content analytics solutions. Using predictive analytics, it reviewed the responses gained from online product reviews by customers, open-ended survey questionnaires, and competitor websites.

In addition to that, it tapped into the insights provided by unbiased, unsolicited client feedback, and this empowered the managers to clearly identify why specific customers were brand detractors or brand promoters. The firm was also able to enhance their customer satisfaction rates and product development as well as increase its marketing effectiveness. The executives of the company now continued to monitor newsfeeds, blogs, and other sources from which they could review public opinion of their products and services.

Understanding the Affinities between Customers and Products

Majority of retailers continuously try to identify as well as analyse the past and present buying behaviour of customers. They do this to predict future trends that will successfully drive enhanced customer profitability and loyalty.

Business analytics enables organizations to identify the purchasing behaviour of consumers by mining into the historical and the real-time data to reveal bits of useful information, such as affinities between the products, between customers, as well as the combination of the two.

Together with this information, you will be able to view past the prevailing trends and set the stage for your company's future outcomes.

Advanced Affinity Analysis

Retailers can gain an insight into the buying patterns of consumers by conducting an affinity analysis. This helps them to match their products, services, and promotions with the preferences and behaviour of shoppers while also linking purchases to particular buyers in order to develop tailored offers.

Retailers can execute more precise and targeted campaigns to drive greater returns for an enhanced bottom line.

This type of analysis can aid decisions and processes that are executed in or across any of the channels, which is especially important for the retailers that operate a multiple or omnichannel company.

Market Basket Analysis

The affinity analysis also incorporates the market basket analysis, a type of analysis that utilises algorithms to analyse the individual customer data points, transactions, purchasing history, and a lot more information and builds various predictive models that can be used to
- ✓ determine whether an offer is valid for a specific type of customers or a certain group of customers,
- ✓ decide which categories of products need to be displayed or promoted together,
- ✓ predict the chances that the consumer will positively respond to the promotion/offer, and
- ✓ calculate the value of the customers responding to the offer.

Understanding Customer Preferences

The analysis conducted through these methods also enables the retailer to comprehend preferences of customers based on segmentation, product correlations, along with affinities from market basket analysis. It is also able to generate numerous scenarios and offers and determines the possibility of customers responding to the offers and promotions. The analysis empowers retail organizations to opt for the next best action for their consumers, develop loyalty within that customer, and increase the revenues together with margins for the company.

Anticipating the Consumers' Next Move

Predictive insight provides insight that assists retailers in anticipating what the customers are likely to do next, which of them are probably going to move onto the competitor, or which group of customers will respond to the cross-sell and upsell campaigns in a positive manner.

Predictive insight can also identify the areas of potential risk and fraud or spot opportunities in new and emerging markets. Retail companies that automate and optimise the decisions that are informed by the predictive analysis gain a considerable advantage over their competition.

Improving Your Retail Promotions

The cost of promotional and marketing campaigns can have a considerable impact on any retailer's bottom line. By applying the collected insights through business analytics, your retail organization can gain a competitive advantage while making sure it protects its gains.

For instance, business analytics enables managers to effectively plan advertising and marketing campaigns, model and then evaluate all the possible promotion options (depending on the sales lift), monitor the results, and analyse offers to ensure optimal returns on their investment.

Business analytics is able to provide a spontaneous bottom-up and top-down planning as well as a reporting environment to enable marketers to understand what kind of impact their promotional programs have on the company's finances.

CHAPTER 8: MAKING SMART BUSINESS DECISIONS

Smart merchandising decision-making involves two aspects. Firstly, it requires a retailer to **understand and predict the customers' needs and wants.** Secondly, it expects the retailer to do so while **controlling the costs.** This is because a company can conduct all the research it wants, but this costs money. Unless the research provides valuable insights that can help the company improve its revenue, there is no point in carrying out unending research and analysis of the market and the consumers.

Apart from checking the feasibility of an analysis and research, the retailer also has to make sure that the data it gains through its efforts to understand the customers must be used effectively to make crucial business decisions that are to have an impact on the company's bottom line.

If all this sounds like an intimidating task, then it well may be. Unless your firm is able to effectively tap into the power and benefits of

RANDOM FACT
It has become a necessity for businesses to continuously review business analytics and utilize relevant tools to understand the latest trends and demands of the modern consumer. The companies that do not make efforts to get an insight into consumer behaviour eventually fall way behind in the intense competition.

business analytics, the entire ordeal can turn out to be loss-yielding. But if you have not figured it out, **business analytics is the best friend of any retailer**.

There is no denying the fact that business analytics is transforming the way retailers make decisions amid multitudes of complex data, including the sentiments of customers and their responses to the actions of retailers. All this helps retailers like you to understand what the consumers want so that you can develop and supply the products based on the demand of consumers, providing the correct quantities through the right types of channels. When this is done right, you will be setting yourself as a leader within your industry, standing out from your competitors in terms of building loyalty, trust, and brand advocacy.

This chapter focuses on helping you create new efficient merchandising plans, enhance current merchandising plans, and more.

Enabling Your Merchandising Efficiencies

In the merchandising efficiencies realm, business analytics is a boon, as the applications and technologies can make your company much more efficient, mainly through the following four functions:
- ✓ By **predicting consumer demand**
- ✓ Through **financial and operational retail planning**
- ✓ By **minimizing markdowns and stock-outs**
- ✓ By **optimizing assortment**

Business analytics is able to help merchandising teams dynamically alter and tailor the assortments by providing actionable insights. The assortments can be tailored based on upcoming trends, consumer purchasing patterns, and location and demographic insights.

Additionally, by implementing what is learned from affinity analysis, you can continue to refine what you should stock with an understanding of not just the individual product performance but also of the cross-sell potential. There are some product affinities that may be affected by current events or seasonality. Hence, you will have the flexibility to enhance the shopping experience of customers for varying demographics while you continue to provide new opportunities to focus on the specific products or combinations of products that get the highest profits, greatest margins, and strongest consumer loyalty.

Integration of merchandising, assortments, and the supply chain within the initiatives that are propelled by marketing is crucial as many retailers struggle to develop brand experience for their customers.

RANDOM FACT

Merchandising teams can greatly benefit from business analytics as it can help them alter and tailor the assortments by equipping them with insights that are truly actionable.

Merchandisers can tailor assortments based on consumer purchasing patterns, upcoming trends, and location and demographic insights.

It all boils down to having the right kind of product at the right time, and this can only be understood through collecting and understanding customer analytics. All the activities mentioned in the last few chapters are crucial to a company's success as they keep it aligned with the needs of customers, whatever they may be. Developing an environment where merchandising can rapidly adjust to the changing needs of the customer, their response, and their behaviour is what every retailer should aim to develop. This environment will also empower the retailers to not only optimise their supply chain but also enhance the inventory position while minimizing markdowns and protecting margins.

Reuniting Bottom-Up and Top-Down Plans

Reuniting bottom-up and top-down plans is a great challenge for a number of retailers. A business analytics solution for the purpose of assortment planning can offer such retailers a way to develop consensus, allowing them to synchronise plans.

For instance, depending on their targets, the retailers can create top-down retail financial plans by category or by department. They may also create bottom-up plans for stores, channels, or even clusters of different stores. The retailers can customise or preset the profiles for the basic as well as the seasonal merchandise. These preset seasonality profiles can assist the retailers in promoting seasonal or promotional product stocks.

Creating Dynamic Retail Assortments

You can manage assortments through business analytics to align demand plans and merchandise plans as well as financial plans that will help you develop an item-level, dynamic assortment at channel, division, category, and department levels. By enabling such processes, you will be able to analyse and comprehend the differences in plans while developing specific what-if scenarios to gain an understanding of their impact on the key performance indicators and corporate goals.

After your bottom-up and top-down plans have been reconciled, a stock plan can manage the inventory levels as well as the key metrics.

Retail organizations are then able to
- compare the results to their plans,
- analyse their in-season sales data,
- reforecast as required to meet the demand of customers and the conditions of the market,
- perform scenario-planning in a 'sandbox' environment to figure out how to manage sudden changes in the current market,
- receive any alerts that support the workflow, and
- implement changes, such as costs or targets, which should be immediately available to all the concerned stockholders.

This approach provides many benefits, including the following:
- Applicable information regarding the changes in demand, targets, costs, or supply constraints can be collectively used when working with the same dynamic plans.
- The impact is almost immediately visible to all the stakeholders.
- Action can be taken in a timely manner to make sure that the retailer taps into the latest opportunities and manages issues constructively.

Bringing into Line the Store-Level Assortment with the Demand

It is unlikely to have the same product demand in every store. Simplistic segmentation—including age, location, store size, or layout—does not consider the unique store characteristics or account differentiators.

To keep up with customer demand and inventory of their stores, retailers need to understand the purchase patterns for each of their stores and through stock-keeping units, or SKU. Predicting assortment and sales at an individual SKU-level and then developing plans to make smart investment decisions for inventory are some of the most crucial capabilities retailers must be equipped with.

A latest retail study[7] has revealed that almost a 10 per cent reduction on low-volume SKUs can lead to a 4 per cent increase in sales because of the space reallocation. Retailers, when equipped with store-level assortment analytics, are able to accurately predict the prospect of selling specific products by a particular store for a certain period of time. Ultimately, this helps them in effectively meeting the demands of their customers while optimizing inventory levels. Hence, the sales increase, and the inventory costs continue to decrease.

> **RANDOM FACT**
> Retailers that equip themselves with store-level assortment analytics are much more capable of making accurate predictions when it comes to predicting the possibility of selling certain products at a particular store during a certain time period.

Advanced analytics automate this entire process by developing a unique predictive model for every other SKU in a retailer's portfolio. Here is how it works:

Each model effectively assesses the impact of any possible predictors that are available to specific retailer on product, store, environmental conditions, or category.

These individual models are developed to allow for an exclusive relationship at the store level and between each of the products, matching how the product and the managers of each category perceive the world.

This approach also complements the organization's decision-making process by controlling the sheer number of all products at the same time it develops detailed local influences, which are mostly lost at the higher planning levels.

The advantage of having an intelligent assortment planning forecast is that it clearly identifies the items that have the highest probability of being sold at the greatest margin. As a result of this, retailers are capable of creating detailed and dynamic merchandising plans with efficient assortments, which elevate sales, provide the retailer a competitive advantage, and ultimately result in greater customer satisfaction rates.

Business analytics for assortment planning goes well beyond the traditional limitations of ERP systems, spreadsheets, and many custom software that require considerable technical support in order to
- create a differentiated assortment;
- protect profits and make smart buys;
- comprehend the trends and respond effectively to the changing market trends and factors;
- understand the financial impact of the business decisions and model scenarios;
- effectively control the level of stock and enhance inventory investments;
- provide logistics support with precise requirements, thereby getting rid of the need to redistribute excess stock; and
- increase wallet share and customer satisfaction.

Developing Supply Chain Driven by Demand

Analytics tools can help you develop a demand-driven supply chain. Keeping in mind that an average retailer's assets are normally over 70 per cent inventory, improving the demand forecast accuracy at SKU-level, and reducing quantity of inventory can greatly contribute to a better balance sheet.

> **RANDOM FACT**
> Technology has greatly enhanced supply chain management and empowered retailers to keep track of each and every aspect of their supply chain.
>
> Retailers should try to avoid making any shortcuts when it comes to managing their supply chain as an effective stock will directly affect the company's bottom line.

Is there a problem of being out of stock at your retail stores? Do you have to manage excess inventory that eventually has to be returned to the supplier, discarded, or perhaps sold at an expensive markdown? If you've answered yes to any of the

---

7 *'The Value of Smarter Merchandising', IBM, SOURCE.*

questions above, you should use technology to support your planning processes to effectively control such cases.

By controlling the levels and offerings of the inventory to your near real-time customer insight and performance analysis, you can protect your company's working capital and increase the return on investment. Meanwhile, you will note that your customer satisfaction level will increase along with the number of customers as they will be able to find their products when they want it and where they want it.

Making Use of Proven Technology

There are numerous types of tools that can help you collect the crucial analytics data regarding the demand of products and any ongoing trends. For instance, we have discussed the iConnect Wi-Fi analytics tool in the previous chapters of this book. Wi-Fi analytics tools and modern Wi-Fi infrastructures help retailers by providing in-depth information regarding the behaviour of customers while transforming the customers' in-store experience in the following five ways:

1. Empowering customers to self-service whenever in the store
2. Increasing customer loyalty and retention
3. Line busting and mobile point-of-sale
4. Displaying advertising and digital signage
5. Providing support for a number of Wi-Fi-enabled devices in-store

Empowering Customers to Self-Service Whenever in the Store

Successful retailers know the value of the Wi-Fi analytics tools. They know that by providing Internet access to their customers, they can empower the customers to check the details of a product, check availability in the aisle, and check the gift registry.

Once the customers are in your store, the convenience of having the ability to order or purchase something instantly enhances the shopping satisfaction. It can also avail personalised offers or loyalty programs while using their mobile device for finding their way. With the consumers in your store's network, you can persuade them to use your website or a mobile app (if it is available) to use online services, join an online community, or get them to promote on social media channels.

As has been previously mentioned, the number of individuals who carry a mobile device that has its Wi-Fi ON has increased dramatically. Depending on the type of store and the consumer demographics, between 40 and 70 per cent of all the customers carry a phone with its Wi-Fi capability switched on. With the right type of wireless network and the analytics software, you can use the signals emitted from their phones to accurately track and determine their behaviour and derive many other useful analytical data.

A simple Wi-Fi connection for your customers can be transformed into a full-fledged business analytics tool that is capable of representing the foot traffic inside and outside the store. These tools will help you optimise your entire retail operations while enhancing per-store revenue. A Wi-Fi tool can allow you to do the following:

- **Optimise your capture rate**–You can optimise your capture rate and increase your sales per day. Identify the shopping apps that consumers use and collect the number of walk-bys and visits of customers and the percentage of the people that actually come inside your store.
- **Increase the duration rates**—You can track the duration of each customer's visit or work out an average. Identify the shoppers that stay longer than a certain period of time to determine

engagements. This data can then be used to tailor your store's sales process and enhance store operations.

- **Improve the service levels**—Monitor length of queues, salesperson availability, and the time it takes for a salesperson to engage with a customer to improve the quality of service.
- **Improve the engagement level with customers**—The analytics data collected through the Wi-Fi network can be used to track traffic patterns, personalise in-store coupons and offers, and assess effectiveness of your promotions while allowing you to capture data for maximizing the effectiveness of social media.
- **Improve customer retention and loyalty**—Track the walk-by and walk-in frequency by repeat visits and recent visits to determine leading customers and then use the information to develop effective loyalty programs.

Increasing Customer Loyalty and Retention

An increasing number of retailers are starting to believe that a mobility solution, such as the iConnect Shopper Intelligence Analytics, is crucial to improving their brand and consumer loyalty. It helps them integrate their sales channels as effectively as possible. For instance, they can incorporate particular features such as shipping certain products to the customer's home or to the nearest store while unifying the customer's shopping cart.

The data that is gathered across multiple channels provides for a holistic view of the consumer and enhances the number of opportunities for cross-selling and upselling. This 'unification of channels' is known as *omnichannel integration* among retailers and businesses, and Wi-Fi is the critical component of any omnichannel integration. In this manner, stores can stay connected with their customers and reduce the possibility of an incomplete purchase while building loyalty through supple channel offerings.

Line Busting and Mobile Point-of-Sale

The 'anywhere, anytime' model offered by mobile is undoubtedly its greatest asset. However, when retail is concerned, no location is more important than the space right next to the customer. More and more retailers are now starting to focus on providing constant attention to shoppers through Wi-Fi-enabled devices in order to be able to answer their questions, provide quality customer service, and effectively try to complete purchase transaction.

By empowering the store employees to move from checkout aisles to be next to the prospective customer in order to complete a transaction is what retailers refer to as line busting. The experience of a customer is greatly enhanced when a transaction is completed over a Wi-Fi network using a mobile POS device as it eliminates the need to stand in a queue.

Displaying Advertising and Digital Signage

Traditionally, retailers had lured customers by handing out advertisement leaflets or by displaying static display advertisements made of paper or plastic, and these ads were normally updated every week or so. These ads were distributed by the headquarters of a retail chain without any space for any customization by a franchisee store or a local store.

With a modern Wi-Fi-enabled store network, you as a retailer can now display digital signage on smart TVs. With such flat-panel TVs available in all kinds of sizes, retailers now have an option to install them at as many vantage points as needed to draw the attention of customers.

When the correct type of Wi-Fi network is implemented, a rich multimedia experience can be effectively delivered to the customers.

Providing Support for a Number of Wi-Fi-Enabled Devices In-Store

Wi-Fi has transformed the way mobile devices in retail stores connect to the available network. They have ushered PCI compliance, flexibility, and the reliability of conventional tethered devices. Conventional retail stores can be divided into three distinct zones:
1. Checkout and POS zone
2. Executive and store manager zone
3. Distribution area and back-end warehouse

Each of these zones has some form of device that is used for a number of different purposes, such as coupon printers, product scanners, and payment registers in the first zone, laptops and tablets in the second, and computerised forklifts and other equipment in the third.

The right type of Wi-Fi network will support a wide range of devices for the entire operation of the store besides providing crucial analytics pertaining to customers.

> **RANDOM FACT**
> As a store owner, you can benefit greatly by providing your customers with FREE Wi-Fi access. Everyone loves free stuff, and free Wi-Fi is an added benefit.

Getting to Grips with Supply Chain Challenges

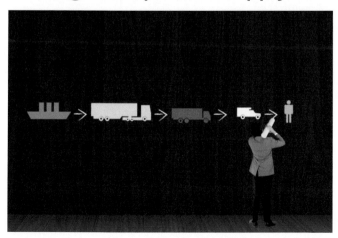

Supply chain challenges are not new to the retail world; however, managing the supply chain at times when retailers are trying to provide an *omnichannel shopping experience* to customers in order to boost their sales and customer retention rates is, indeed, a challenge.

Supply chain challenges can range from unexpected bottlenecks to miscommunications with suppliers to inaccurate forecasts that lead to out of stocks or overstocks. As a result, retailers are faced with a concoction of data challenges that are simply multiplied with the integration of multiple channels for customers. If such challenges are not handled with utmost care, it can seriously jeopardise the ability of the retailer to offer its customers a seamless shopping experience.

Ensuring that your customers are getting the products when they want it and where they want it is absolutely critical in maintaining an acceptable level of satisfaction and in enhancing customer loyalty.

Supply chain challenges can quite easily make a customer switch over to your competitor; hence, retailers are increasingly becoming interested in ensuring how they can effectively manage their supply chain–related issues while providing their customers a seamless omnichannel shopping experience.

Getting Visibility across the Supply Chain

If you cannot see it, you cannot fix it. This is the basic concept behind solving supply chain issues. To improve the shopping experience of your customers and to be able to meet their demands, you need to focus on key metrics throughout the supply chain, including sales, inventory, labour, and deliveries (both in transit and forecasted).

Here are some ways business analytics helps management of supply chain:
- It helps by lowering the costs and improving margins by maintaining a reliable supply chain management process, which itself is based on integrated analysis of data from a number of different systems.
- It can help by delivering a cross-functional insight that assists businesses to analyse their spending and the performance of the supplier swiftly and cost-effectively.
- It can help by ensuring that the products are sourced to enhance purchasing power by comprehending relative procurement patterns from KPIs, or key performance indicators.

Solving Operational Problems before They Occur

When operations managers have the ability to look into performance issues in detail, they are able to get right to the root of a particular problem and effectively resolve it before it gets any worse. Timely problem-solving is key to maintaining and providing a seamless shopping experience for the customers along with reducing costs due to any bottlenecks in supply chain or inaccurate forecasts. It also plays a crucial role in enhancing customer service.

In operations, retailers use business analytics in the following three ways:
- Reporting performance and opening and closing of stock position by division, channel, store, region, or account as well as product or category, using comparisons and benchmarking between specific periods in an attempt to identify the potential for improvements to the overall efficiency.
- Analysing traffic data and sales transactions to understand the demand, build forecasts to meet the demands, and improve the in-stock position while reducing any out-of-stock or overstock situations. The performance of a retailer is increased when it has the right products at the right location, according to the needs of the customer. This also reduces the customer service challenges faced by the retailer, along with the call centre needs, while enhancing brand loyalty with the customers.
- Keeping retail operations in complete alignment with the marketing and merchandising efforts in order to solidify the customer experience. Whenever the customer-facing employees are properly aligned with the cross-organizational targets, performance, plans, and targets, the employees are in a better position to educate their customers about the marketing promotions and initiatives while keeping the stock and inventory levels into account. Same results can be achieved when customers make a purchase online by automating analysis and integration of data points and providing optimised propositions. All this results in a greater and more pleasant shopping experience for the company's customers.

Collaborating with the Vendors

Vendors are a key component in the value chain of any retailer. Retailers can work in collaboration with the vendors to provide performance sharing and visibility and to develop forecast to enable the latter to enhance their upstream processes. This, in turn, makes the vendors more capable of meeting the retailer's demands for delivery while cutting costs throughout the value chain. If a certain vendor's processes and systems are adequately advanced, the data regarding daily and store-level transactions provides an agile answer to unexpected changes in customer demand. It also leads to a greater accuracy in forecasting as compared to a scenario where only the aggregated data has been shared.

Performance against the service level agreements together with transactional data can be mutually used through electronic methods or certain automated routes.

This can also act as a portal for providing various performance benchmarks to the vendors, providing encouragement so that they meet the high standards of the industry's leading vendors. This teamwork between the retailer and vendor can determine the exact causes of performance that is below the target and also encourages integration of methods for further optimization and enhancement.

Managing Brand Loyalty

Brand loyalty—two words that hold the potential to make any retail organization worth millions of dollars. For long-term success of your organization, brand loyalty is crucial for many reasons, as follows:

- ✓ *Brand loyalty* augments the lifetime value of each of your customers.
- ✓ *Brand loyalty* transforms your consumers into brand marketers through social media posts, word-of-month marketing, and product reviews.
- ✓ *Brand loyalty* increases the overall number of sales per customer.

> **RANDOM FACT**
> Loyal customers tend to consistently buy from their preferred brands, regardless of the price they pay or the level of convenience offered.

Customers loyal to a brand give useful feedback on what your retail organization is doing right and what it isn't doing right, along with information such as what needs to be done to make things right. It is not easy at all to build and maintain brand loyalty; however, the **secret to building brand loyalty lies in providing utmost customer satisfaction.**

Retailers have learnt something very crucial in the last economic downturn. They have realised that keeping a current customer is a lot easier than trying to make a new one. However, beyond customer retention programs and loyalty, the role of business analytics is a crucial one in assisting retailers in understanding what needs to be done in order to develop brand loyalty.

Building Brand Loyalty in the Digital Era

In today's digital era, where omnichannel shopping experience is becoming widespread, it has become quite a challenge to manage brands to drive loyalty and to develop a cohesive and compelling customer experience. To fully understand the driving force behind brand loyalty, retail organizations need to answer the following questions:

- ✓ **Which of our customers are not satisfied?**
- ✓ **What efforts do we make to retain our loyal consumers?**
- ✓ **Can we attempt to fix our relationship with unhappy customers and transform them into loyal ones?**

Driving brand loyalty is not just about maintaining a rewards system that depends on the cash spent by customers or their number of visits. Today's modern consumer wants a customised experience at every point right up to the point of purchase, ranging from awareness to the engagement to the actual sale and beyond. The only way to retain customers effectively is by analysing data to develop a clear understanding of their changing expectations.

Business analytics gathered by analytics tools, such as Wi-Fi Shopper Intelligence Analytics, are highly effective in providing retailers an insight into those channels that are ideal for engaging specific customers at particular points throughout the purchase process. The latest technologies offer evidence into what types of products your consumers are attracted to, which products they account become interested in, together with information on which marketing efforts are yielding results, and which offer should be made to accomplish a sale and satisfy the needs of the customer.

When the capabilities of business intelligence and advanced analytics are combined, retail organizations can effectively uncover the trends and patterns of their customers' behaviour and feelings and then use that data to derive and forecast future outcomes by making quicker and smarter decisions.

Data and results of the analysis can be quickly delivered to relevant decision makers through the use of scorecards, reports, and dashboards, or they can even be fed directly into the company's marketing automation tools, automatically triggering the appropriate action.

By their self-learning the predictive models, it can be ensured that each iteration of the consumer is more accurate than before.

The Challenges of Building Brand Loyalty

Even though it is easier to retain a current customer than make a new one, this does not at all imply that customer retention is any easier. Retailers have to remain on their toes in an attempt to retain their valuable customers and prevent situations where they are likely to lose them to their competitors. Keep in mind the following statistics:
- ✓ Of the respondents of the survey, 56 per cent were somewhat prone to switching brands based on the retail organization's customer service options.
- ✓ Women are 10 per cent less likely to feel loyalty towards a particular brand than men.
- ✓ In the US, 25 per cent of adults do not feel loyalty for any type of brand at all.

Consumers often switch from one brand to another for a number of reasons, including special promotions, pricing, poor customer service, and convenience, to name a few. In some instances, customers have to make a switch because a particular store does not have a certain product in stock or because the customers' current brand does not provide them an omnichannel experience.

The good thing is that retailers can discover the negative trends in the sale of their products through business analytics. By knowing what is causing a leak in their sales funnel, they can work to patch up the leak and restore their buoyancy.

Business analytics also helps you gain insights from your range of products and services that are doing well in terms of sales and customer satisfaction rates. Additionally, business analytics also provides tools that enable retailers to build solid brand loyalty through better offerings, better customer services, better promotions and prices, and a number of other factors.

RANDOM FACT
It is not easy for brands to instill loyalty among customers, particularly with so many competitors on the horizon.

However, with the right approach, businesses can gather data, analyse it, and use it to build loyalty in a manner that keeps the customers hooked on to the company's products and services no matter what.

Putting the Data to Use

A recent study of chief marketing officers carried out by IBM has disclosed that developing and sustaining brand loyalty among their customers are the top priority of today's CMOs. However, despite this, almost 72 per cent feel as if they are not properly prepared to build loyalty for their brands. Around 70 per cent of these CMOs are also concerned about the huge data explosion. They have on their hands complex data that they need to make sense of. They get this data from a number of sources, such as tweets, consumer blogs, videos, and texts. So much data can be overpowering, to say the very least.

The proliferation of mobile devices and social media is leading to a new, complex breed of consumers that are technology-savvy and have the skills and the know-how to compare and quickly evaluate the products and services that meet their needs. Sharp marketing professionals are drawing in as much of this information as they can to gain useful insight from the sources mentioned above, including social media as a whole, and are incorporating the data into their marketing strategies for positive outcomes.

When it comes to predicting what the customers will want, the key lies in adapting those marketing strategies that will offer them the things they need, where they want it, and at what price. Business analytics is a powerful means of providing you all the insights you need to start building brand loyalty.

Meeting the Needs of Today's Consumers

CMOs need to have tools to properly manage the demands of today's consumers that have an instant impact on any brand through Facebook, Twitter, and other social media channels. Almost two-thirds of CMOs in midmarkets are attempting to manage social media's impact on their marketing functions and are struggling to comprehend how their organization can leverage from social media activity.

Many retailers invest a lot of resources in trying to respond to each of the queries from consumers on social media networks but skip conducting a thorough analysis of the same dialogues. Additionally, only less than half of all the midmarket CMOs take their time to gain an understanding of the impact of consumer-generated blogs, reviews, and third-party rankings have on their brand.

Social media analytics tools can assist retailers in positively identifying the emerging business opportunities and the areas that are problematic and direct towards the actions that can solve them effectively and efficiently.

The retail organization should be able to use this data to relate to key performance indicators, such as service levels and sales, and should appropriately prioritise and invest in the right type of action. This process can help increase an organization's return on investment by enhancing customer experience while leading to further improvements across the entire customer base.

The Growth of Mobile Commerce

The growing number of mobile devices and the popularity of social media platforms have resulted in the development of an entirely new breed of consumers who are more demanding and whose needs are in a constant flux.

By 2016, mobile commerce is expected to reach a staggering $31 billion. Unfortunately, as has been mentioned previously, CMOs and other marketing professionals are not prepared to deal with such a rapid increase in the number of devices and channels.

The increase in mobile shopping fuels an increase in the marketing challenges faced by retail organizations and businesses while complicating data collection and analysis. It threatens both customer retention as well as customer service.

Yet again, business analytics comes to the rescue by allowing you to gather mobile data in an attempt to manage your brand better and to provide your consumers with a shipping experience that will ensure long-term loyalty.

Getting Higher ROI on Marketing Investments

Marketing officers are now held accountable financially by their organizations and are expected to produce greater business outcomes at a faster rate than ever before. Even though CMOs commonly believe that the return on investment on the dollars they have spent on marketing is the most crucial measuring stick for figuring out the success of their organization by the end of 2015, a study conducted by IBM[8] has revealed that almost 72 per cent of all CMOs are grossly underprepared when it comes to effectively managing the sharp decline in brand loyalty. Business analytics is capable of instantly showing which marketing campaigns are actually generating business for the company and which are not doing so well, allowing marketers to adjust and modify them before higher losses are incurred.

Developing Trust with Customers

Besides the current economic conditions, an even bigger factor that impacts brand loyalty is present. The rapid innovations in technology, the increasing competition due to this technology, and the widespread popularity of

social networking have equipped people with tools they can use to discover, compare, evaluate, choose, and experience brands. With the escalation in the use and the numbers of social media networks, together with the need for increased transparency, personal exchanges and trust between the marketplace and the consumer are now resulting in the formation of keystone of all marketing efforts.

Analytical data can assist organizations in communicating their marketing messages and promotions that actually resonate with the targeted audience. When used properly, the data collected can actually instil and ignite brand loyalty in your consumers.

In addition, when the entire company is aligned around the concept of consumer satisfaction, which will ultimately lead to customer loyalty, the results can be very positive and build the much-needed trust, which will result in the development of a strong, ongoing relationship between a brand and its customer.

When each part of a particular retail company, ranging from merchandising to marketing to store operations, is aligned in a way that they focus on meeting the needs of the customer, brand loyalty will automatically start to be generated. One way this can be done is by providing the front-line staff of the organization the ability to handle queries of customers properly and by rewarding high-value consumers. These efforts tend to foster brand loyalty continuously.

Managing Performance of a Store

It involves intricate skills on the part of a retailer to balance an increasing number of sales while protecting margins and profits besides ensuring that an outstanding shopping experience is provided to the customers. No area is more crucial than right at the storefront, where the company's planning, preparing, and execution

8 'IBM Global SMO Study', IBM, SOURCE.

play out. After hard work and efforts are focused on these areas, right from the corporate to the actual field, it eventually boils down to the consumer shopping experience through numerous channels.

It is important to keep all the stores integrated into the main planning process while giving the managers of each of the stores access to all the data and the key metrics to ensure that the retail organization can act as a single brand, thereby helping propel customer loyalty.

By providing the people who work at the store level with valuable actionable insights, the entire organization will be ensured to head towards common goals.

In this section, we will learn how business analytics can provide you the ability to effectively integrate and manage the compensation.

Incorporating Stores into a Retail Firm's Planning Process

Limited planning often leads to several breakdowns throughout any retail company. The failure to drive key organizational plans and analytics down to the store level can lead to a much lower number of sales and margins and eventually cause disappointment among customers. In order to enhance the performance of stores, more and more retailers turn towards business analytics to manage and carry out planning of store operations and to tie store management directly to marketing activity, corporate plans, and all the merchandising projections.

Recognizing Ineffective Processes

RANDOM FACT
Ineffective technologies can significantly affect your bottom line and stunt the growth of your business.

It is crucial to understand which processes are outdated and cap the potential of your business.

In most retail organizations, planning cycles tend to be long and dreary, which have to go through multiple iterations, which are hard to merge. The results are often silo-based planning, with each area having its own bottom-up planning (areas such as operations, finance, marketing, and merchandising).

These bottom-up plans do not offer support for any strategic initiatives, nor do they tie into any single group of top-down targets, leading to a misalignment in the company's corporate strategy and the actual execution in the field.

Recognizing Ineffective Technologies

Majority of budgeting, planning, and forecasting solutions have been designed to put forth annual expenditures and revenues based on the performance of a particular period in the past, with the increase or the decrease applied throughout the board. Such plans are not able to provide continuous insights, which are required to correct the course of strategic decisions, or build environments that encourage dynamic planning, nor can they positively encourage and engage influencers and decision makers during the process.

Effectual store planning depends on the proper integration of corporate targets into an organization's marketing plans, which are designed to drive merchandising decisions, as well as assortment plans.

Despite this, many retailers continue to find themselves engrossed in a technological environment that actually reduces efficiency.

✓ Spreadsheets are disconnected, slow, and prone to errors. They develop huge amounts of operational and financial data, with each contributor working independently from their coworkers, and that too in an offline environment. In addition to this, it becomes almost impossible for the information to be quickly consolidated to provide a corporate-wide view.

✓ Constructing what-if models and then evaluating the potential results of plan versus the changes is unwieldy, to say the least, particularly in the traditional-planning environments, which utilise spreadsheets. This eradicates the ability to use insight when making confident and informed decisions with a surety of impact throughout the organization.

✓ General lodger solutions or ERP are not designed to be used when planning down to the granular level of expenses, revenue, initiatives, and labour needed by retailers.

✓ While off-the-shelf solutions may offer a wide range of generic functions, they do not address the particular needs of any retail business, including incorporation of finance into departmental planning in areas such as merchandising, marketing, channel management, and store operations. Whenever complex modelling is needed, the majority of planning and budgeting as well as ERP solutions can literally come to a halt.

Finding a Blueprint for Success

Managing operations of a store through analytics empowers the retailer with a high-volume, high-performance, item-level planning and multidimensional modelling as well as data visualization. It enables the retailer to review data and model the business requirements for the entire organization. The results of analysing the data can then be used for budgeting and forecasting purposes with greater confidence for enhanced business outcomes.

For instance, a retailer may collect information from more individuals, including district, regional, or store managers, more regularly and then tie this information (bottom-up plans) to the top-down targets in order to keep the organization on track and aligned with the main goals.

Business analytics provides for a higher participation, increased accountability, and visibility, together with analytical processing, which automates the contributions from various systems. Planning managers can understand the planning cycle's maturity easily, eliminate any delays in rolling out the plans, and swiftly evaluate the impact of forecasts and plans to make any adjustments.

> ### RANDOM FACT
> Business analytics empowers store managers with the tools and data they need to effectively manage each and every aspect of their store's operations. To unleash the true potential of your business in today's highly competitive environment, you need to ensure that you take every step possible to gain an edge over your competitors.

CHAPTER 9: UNDERSTANDING SOCIAL MEDIA IN RETAIL

Social media has transformed the way we connect to others, how we share and shape our relationships with people and entire communities from all over the world. The world of social media is moving rapidly, and retailers and brands are now beginning to understand the importance of leveraging the social media scene together with its users while determining how they will be playing their role to gain a greater presence in their respective markets.

Today's consumers are connected to brands and retailers like never before, thanks to the implosion of social media networks such as Twitter and Facebook. Brands and retailers can interact with their customers by sharing content generated by users or by creating blog posts and videos. This tends to create new opportunities for businesses and brands to use social media to their advantage across the entire value chain. However, the challenge lies in determining the ideal time and the approach that needs to be taken to turn any ongoing conversations on social media into an enhanced shopping experience for customers.

In addition to that, the considerable impact of feedback from customers has never been as strong as it is now: it reaches out to businesses much quicker and spreads to a very broad audience because of social media. Social media has empowered the consumer to a level never achieved in the entire history of retail.

How It All Begins

If businesses wish to understand the impact of social media channels on retail, the very first step will be to understand the origin of social media and the role it plays in the lives of people today. Why is it that social media is so addictive? What makes people spend so much of their time on Twitter or Facebook? What do these people do when they are on social media websites?

To start with, it needs to be understood that humans are social beings. Friends, families, and social groups are a crucial part of our lives, and people perish without this bonding. Nevertheless, life has become very hectic, and the amount of time people spend working or commuting from their home to their office and vice versa has increased considerably. Amid the hectic schedule, social media networks make it easy for people to socialise during their busy day whenever they want to.

According to a global firm that provides integrated consumer insight, if the amount of time spent on the Internet for PCs was condensed into an hour, then around 27 per cent of it would have been spent on social networking websites throughout US, Australia, and UK in 2012.

In the United States, almost sixteen minutes of every hour are spent online on social media websites, nine minutes are spent on entertainment websites, and five minutes on shopping. This tells us the importance of the Internet and how it has changed the way we create and share in the community.

Before any retailer or brand creates a Twitter or Facebook account, they need to understand what people actually do during the time they spend on these social hubs. Four behavioural constants in today's social world have been defined by the Coca-Cola Retailing Research Council. These constants are at the heart of the very people that connect on social media:

1. **CREATE**

We tend to gain acceptance and a sense of accomplishment by originating and sharing content that we have approved. This content can take several forms, including that of articles, pictures, blogs, videos, etc.

2. **COMMUNICATE**

We wish to stay in touch with other people. Twitter and Facebook are the most popular platforms that provide the tools that enable us to do what we want: to stay in touch.

3. **COLLABORATE**

We seek help from people and also work towards accomplishing shared goals. We get together to support a particular cause, raise money in crowdfunding websites, conduct research, and support social initiatives and political campaigns.

4. **CONSULT**

We give and we receive information, including opinions and advice. We perform a lot of research before we make a purchase decision, for instance.

The majority of CMOs say that it is a difficult task for them to determine the starting point. Marketers should always keep in mind whenever they are attempting to add social media into their marketing strategy: what is the company trying to accomplish by establishing its presence on social media?

Retailers should spend time to assess ongoing conversations regarding them on social media. They should observe what customers are saying about them, their products, and the shopping experience. After this, the businesses should try to determine what their reputation is and what role they play in the lives of customers. They must understand what opportunities lie before they actually start participating on social media.

The next step involves outlining an effective approach to engage in a conversation. Finally, some brands and retailers develop their own space to allow customers to connect to them, creating an 'as real as it gets', loyalty-building experience.

Customer Involvement

As history tells us, retailers have had to deal with certain seasonal fluctuations and a slow reaction to the new demands of customers within a same season. This has caused them to lose many opportunities. From this perspective, the consumer of today has a lot more options on their hands. Through customer insights, historical trends, and constant feedback from social media networks, the buying plans are much more flexible and accurate.

Quite often, we see new products failing to bridge the gap between what a brand's product development team has assumed will work and what the customers really wants. Nowadays, most creative managers, together with their teams, have developed the notion of greater collaboration with their consumers. They tend to listen to feedback from customers on the existing range of products and services, while some go a step ahead and involve consumers in the creation of new products.

This modern generation of customers seeks gratification specifically customised to their individual needs.

Transparency is a causal factor and is a requirement in customer participation and communication on social media. Whenever customers are able to see for themselves the value of their communication and collaboration on social media, they get motivated to further get engaged with the retailer, brand, or business.

One great example of transparent consumer involvement in the design of new products is Threadless.com. Their concept is fairly simple: anyone who submits a design idea for a T-shirt will be ranked by other people. If the design manages to get a certain number of votes, the shirt will make it to the store, and the designer will be paid. It utilises crowdsourced design concepts for the success of a T-shirt.

Social media is definitely a very powerful platform for involving customers during the product development phase. For instance, Vitaminwater, which is a unit of Coca-Cola, uses their Facebook account to develop new flavours.

The greater engagement there is between a retailer and its customers, the more a sense of ownership and belonging is created among its customers. Social networking has undoubtedly proven to serve as fertile grounds for seamless brands and customer collaboration.

'Likes' Do Not Equate to Sales

Some retailers and brands have become very obsessed with getting as many likes on their social media accounts. However, the problem is that less than 2 per cent of those likes actually imply some form of an active conversation. Without any meaningful engagement between consumer and retailer, a like has no value at all.

The president of ITC Infotech, L. N. Balaji, says in this regard, *'The challenge is whether consumers are able to find a reflection of their comments on social media pages in the new products presented through online and offline sales channels.'*

With that said, will companies and retailers actually be able to effectively translate any ongoing conversations with their consumers into actionable insights?

According to Balaji, if retail companies are to fully leverage social media interaction, then they will *'need to establish a closed-loop ecosystem, create interactions, structured conversations and condition responses. These responses, when run through business intelligence engines, will generate sentiment boards to provide product*

designers with real-time consumer insights. Products developed while keeping these insights in mind would thus bring more and more "wow" moments for the customers to bring them closer to the brand and create a sustainable competitive advantage'.
[Quote end]

In this regard, content is everything, and in order to develop high-quality content that drives customer engagement, retail companies need to listen to what their customers are talking about at a given moment, what their aspirations are, and what worries them. Actionable insights can be derived from this context and not from senselessly gathering likes.

Complaints Gone Viral

Even though social media has enormous potential for businesses and their brands, it can even turn out to be a weapon capable of total annihilation. It can also be a platform that turns any irritated audience into a highly toxic one.

Prior to the advent of social media, annoyed consumers complained over a company's customer service counter or shouted out their dissatisfaction at a salesman in a store. It was contained—it was very contained.

However, today, a single dissatisfied and disgruntled customer can wreak havoc over a company's image. These complaints tend to go viral, and the reputation of every company is constantly being tested.

A famous instance of a complaint going viral over the Internet involved a musician named Dave. The story involved United Airlines, who broke Dave's guitar, which was a checked-in luggage. After spending eight months of contacting the company to get compensation from the company, he received no response. Dave decided to voice his incident in the form of a song. He created a video and posted it on YouTube.

He has a staggering twelve million views on this video, and this has become an example of the new relationship between customers and companies. The 'United Breaks Guitars' is an example of cautionary tales and the impact that corporate indifference can have. Retailers and companies should never stop listening to their customers.

Social media has become a medium that exposes hypocrisy. Many businesses prefer to be authentic than rehearsed as they are aware that being a bit too polished doesn't work any longer. Nevertheless, being sincere doesn't mean being unprepared. On the other hand, community managers must be imparted a lot of training and constantly reminded that they have to be interested in what their customer is saying, and they should respond with utmost transparency to every complaint, small or large.

Maximizing Shopping Experience Using Social Media

Once upon a time, brick-and-mortar retailers felt really threatened by the immense growth of e-commerce websites that offered the same products, sometimes at lower prices, just with a click. Majority of retailers have now chosen a more integrated and optimistic approach by starting to focus on merging their offline and online worlds. Some of these retailers have even begun to understand the importance of maximizing the shopping experience of their customers through outstanding services, excellent interpersonal skills, and pleasant atmospheres. If these cards are played right, brick-and-mortar stores can gain a huge advantage over their online counterparts!

Social media offers price tools to help them accomplish this: bringing the soul of offline world and integrating it into the customers' lives online. Regardless of the size of a business, a decent camera and a smartphone, together with the discipline and passion to regularly post on social media networks, can greatly enhance any retailer's relationship with its customers.

The practical steps to leverage the power of social media websites are as follows. However, do not forget to listen to, understand, and engage with your customers.

- Add pictures that show your shop floor, including window displays and new arrivals, which will make your customers want to go to your store while having a sensory and pleasant experience compared to when shopping online.
- Encourage your customer to either Instagram or live-tweet your store. You can request your loyal customers to leave video messages no longer than thirty seconds whenever they visit your store or purchase something that they are particularly thrilled about. This will encourage amplification as they will definitely forward the video to their followers and retweet.
- Start a blog that offers meaningful content and that encourages insightful interactions. Aim to become a reliable resource of knowledge by giving advice and useful information on new, advanced trends in your field to your customers.
- Get to know more about geolocation apps; make use of Foursquare or tweet the most suitable public transportation options. By doing this, you can simplify the transition for people when they move from the online world to the real world and try to locate your store.
- Recall that one of the four behavioural constants in the social world is collaboration. Think about the ways in which you can give something back to the society.
- People tend to value things more when they are difficult to get and scarce. Retailers can use this to their advantage by adding deadlines for offers or promotions of certain products. Social media can be used to convey these deadlines to get people to act quicker.

There is no business or company that cannot successfully capitalise on what social media has to offer to them, provided that they comprehend what the needs of their customers are. Social media can help by making the shopping experience really attractive. It also fosters loyalty while increasing customer involvement over time. Besides this, it is a never-ending source of feedback. It is about time that businesses, retailers in particular, start to embrace social media platforms with a meaningful and practical purpose unlike before.

CHAPTER 10: EFFECTIVE STORE PERFORMANCE MANAGEMENT

In the retail industry, the real action takes place at the store. This is a fact; however, retail stores typically fail at even the most basic things that can draw customers to their store for their needs. Chain-operated companies provide the manager of a particular store the standards, tools, and guidance to help him or her run the store in a way that increases sales and ensures customer satisfaction. Nonetheless, the factors that actually make any store successful are dependent on how the manager uses the resources provided to him or her.

Store Operations: The Common Challenges

Most retail companies face challenges pertaining to the basic operations of their stores, especially when they try to manage their store in a results-oriented way. Some of the most common challenges these retail companies face are outlined below:

✓ Keeping the store looking good continuously according to the retail company's standards and guidelines

✓ Displaying all the available products with the correct product information and price

✓ Optimization of inventory levels

- ✓ Decreasing shrink
- ✓ Achieving efficiency in the goods flow
- ✓ Optimizing workforce planning and execution

When these challenges are neglected, the consequences retail businesses have to face are falling number of customers and decreasing revenues. To illustrate the interdependencies and complexity of these challenges, we will look at two of them, including out of stock and shrink, and talk about their fundamental causes and the consequences.

Shrink

Shrink is an issue that is constant among almost all the retail firms and is normally a result of theft, the actions of suppliers, and process and pricing failures. Process failures consist of mistakes in the handling of products during stocking and shelving of the goods. They also include failures in ordering, shelving, and forecasting processes.

The consequences of shrink are out of stocks and lost margin. Key management focus can effectively help to instantly reduce shrink by offering the tools as well as the processes needed to manage the replenishment of goods and the flow processes of goods in the retail store, thereby reducing the process failures.

Out of Stock

Incorrect levels of stocks confuse the replenishment systems and tend to create an out-of-stock condition. Some of the other reasons for this include warehousing and stocking problems, issues with manufacturer availability, and management errors. Out-of-stock conditions have a direct impact on the total sales and customer satisfaction. If a product is not on the shelf, most of the customers will go to another store to buy it. Effective management can minimise most of the reasons that lead to out of stock.

As has been mentioned previously, the problems in retail stores result due to a number of different factors. The ultimate key to avoiding these problems lies with the effective usage of varying routines and tools by the active store management.

In addition to that, to be able to effectively manage the store by facts rather than by opinion, specific traits are needed.

A combination of an analytical mindset and an action-focused style of management can greatly enhance the performance of a store. Analysing key performance indicators (KPIs) and then taking actions based on the store's performance, communicating efficiently, using daily management tools in a systematic way, and clearly allocating roles and responsibilities are all tried-and-tested methods that can help improve store performance.

The Fundamental Elements for Successful Daily Store Management

In order to successfully manage any retail store on a daily basis, certain sets of elements and tools are needed, which must be used systematically to accomplish common goals at all levels throughout the store. These tools must be simple enough for all the store's employees to understand as well as use; however, they should be sophisticated enough to bring about relevant information and the basic structure for decision-making.

The tools and routines mentioned below make for an ideal combination for the purpose of effective store management.

Roles and Responsibilities

Every individual in the store must know what his roles and responsibilities are. There are cases when the individual roles and responsibilities are not clearly documented, defined, or communicated throughout the organizational structure.

Unclear or undefined roles and responsibilities result in the staff making their own decisions regarding what they should be doing. By equipping them with a clear understanding of their roles and responsibilities, which are supported by certain guidelines or rules, you will be making sure that the entire store's staff works together towards common goals.

It is crucial for stores to define roles as well as responsibilities. Equally important is to ensure that each and every one working at the store knows what is expected of him and what he should do to fulfil that expectation. This requires that daily, weekly, quarterly, and annual responsibilities and tasks should be clearly defined, together with key performance indicators and reporting responsibilities, to make sure there are no overlaps or gaps.

When it comes to daily tasks, the roles and responsibilities of each individual help him focus on the correct things so that he can have a positive impact on the growth and success of the store; not only this, but it also serves as a powerful motivator for the employees.

With that said, you must start by clearly defining the roles and responsibilities while communicating them properly to add value to the store's performance.

Daily Management Routines

Efficient daily management routines are designed to focus on ensuring that the basic aspects of running a store are in place and that the employees effectively make immediate improvements whenever needed to enhance store performance. The daily management routines of a retail store, together with its processes, must be executed in a disciplined and systematic manner at each level of the organization.

These daily management routines are critical because in retail environments, things happen quickly, and stores must be equipped to respond to these rapid changes in a quick and effective manner.

Unfortunately, many stores have problems reacting quickly to any changing conditions, particularly those who lack a disciplined and systematic way to make sure that all the day-to-day issues are looked after by the employees. This problem actually originates from a lack of proper usage of tools and poor management skills.

Daily routines tend to simplify everyday tasks that need to be performed to streamline store operations. They offer a guide for the daily work and the management efforts, and as a result, they save considerable time, and the stress and confusion among employees is greatly reduced or even eliminated.

Ordering, cleaning, shelving, and merchandising are some of the daily routines that ensure that the appearance of the store is up to the standards of the organization, the shelves are stocked with products, and the shopping is easy and enjoyable for the customers.

Specific tools, such as task lists or checklists, can also be of a great help to departmental and store managers to ensure everything has been done successfully as is needed.

Key Performance Indicators and Reporting Structure

A store can only be effectively managed when its performance is analysed thoroughly through key performance indicators. Each individual in the retail organization must take responsibility for the performance of the store,

www.shutterstock.com · 222665848

particularly for the areas that can be influenced by their daily actions.

For instance, sales personnel have a direct impact on the daily performance indicators, such as the sales of their department, the sales per man-hour, and the average purchase rates. However, it is unfortunate to see that many stores do not pursue the daily-level KPIs. The reason may be that their employees are not aware of what KPIs are or how the KPIs are linked to their everyday tasks or, perhaps, how they can have an impact on the performance of the store.

Stores must have well-defined KPIs that can be linked with the goals of the store, which can also be broken down to a daily level.

Training at every level of the organization is needed to teach employees the importance of KPIs and how they can use them to determine their input for the growth of the company.

Without an efficient reporting system in place together with the correct KPIs, a retail store may be proceeding in the wrong direction without realizing it, ultimately causing serious problems with profitability.

The time cycle in retail is very short, and therefore, it is essential to control all aspects on a daily level so relevant actions can be taken to counter any problems before they aggravate.

RANDOM FACT
KPIs of any store must match their goals, including long-term and short-term goals, which can be broken down into daily, weekly, and monthly objectives.

Effective Meetings

Store and departmental managers must take steps to run their stores in the most effective manner possible to ensure optimal performance. Internal meetings should be held with the aim of driving performance as well as enhancing customer experience to optimise the store's performance.

The meeting should focus on the improvement actions that need to be taken and basic action logs to help them follow a systematic follow-up of any performance issues.

Above all, these meetings will help support and ultimately drive correct behaviours to ensure continuous improvements of the store.

CHAPTER 11: UNDERSTANDING THE BRICK-AND-MORTAR– ONLINE RETAILER GAP

The emergence and the increased popularity of e-commerce as well as mobile commerce have significantly altered the way in which brands reach out to their customers. It has made it much easier and faster for the consumers to make a purchase, even when on the go, while avoiding all the hassles associated with visiting a physical store.

This has resulted in a tremendous gain in the level of convenience; however, a very crucial aspect linked with any purchase has been lost. This occurs when the human element is removed from the shopping experience offered to consumers.

As e-commerce becomes the mainstream method of shopping, people have started to become accustomed to forfeiting various benefits that they have previously enjoyed with shopping through traditional means. This pursuit of simplicity has, therefore, not led to the ultimate solution and shopping experience.

As an increasing number of individuals seek alternatives to the traditional brick-and-mortar retail stores, it is time for such stores to offer an enhanced shopping experience that combines the best of both worlds. The gap between these two retail channels has to be bridged, and the benefits of both must be combined together to offer something unique and pleasant for today's consumers.

Some of the statistics that highlight the importance of bridging the gap are as follows:
- A study conducted by *Internet Retailer* has projected that mobile commerce sales will double by the end of 2015.[9]
- Forbes predicts that e-commerce sales in the US will increase to over $414 billion by 2018.[10]
- Some brick-and-mortar giants, such as Nordstrom and Macy's, are increasing their efforts to integrate the latest technologies into in-store operations as a result of a drop in their store sales to alternate online shopping channels.

We live in a world where intense competition drives brands to continuously innovate and give their customers improved products, highly customizable options, and a number of different purchasing channels for them to choose from. E-commerce undoubtedly offers numerous benefits over brick-and-mortar stores, such as increased convenience and the ability to comparison-shop. However, the online shopping experience can be taken to a whole new level when technology is embedded into traditional brick-and-mortar stores to offer something that e-commerce alone cannot achieve.

Is this really possible? Yes, it is.

Through proper utilization of technology, the benefits of person-to-person contact can be tapped into.

There are several ways in which businesses and retail stores can escalate the impact of e-commerce and leverage its umpteen benefits. Digital technologies can be implemented to enable personal interactions between the customers and the business. For instance, one way is to develop mobile point of sales (POS) inside retail stores by equipping the sales associates with tablets for easy and quick purchasing, thereby eliminating the need for customers to go through the hassle of getting into a queue to check out.

There are also solutions for the stores that lose their customers to online retailers, such as Amazon, even after the customers have browsed through the physical store. A retailer can invest into mobile app development as well as employee training to ensure that the physical benefits of their store are not lost due to the immense convenience of hassle-free online shopping.

A place that has the greatest potential when it comes to innovation is the apparel industry. The apparel industry probably has the highest barriers to entry into the online shopping arena. However, technologies are now making it possible for such businesses to effectively track all purchases of each of their customers, allowing them to bring the consumer's closet online.

Once a business begins to understand the preferences of their consumers, record purchases, and constantly keep track of the sizing and fit profiles, it becomes easier to predict what a customer will buy in the future. This, on its own, can drive sales significantly; however, there remains a challenge of replacing the physical experience of actually trying out a fabric. This is where brick-and-mortar stores prevail; by offering customers the ability to physically try on the clothing, they provide them an experience unmatched by online shopping. This is precisely why the brick-and-mortar stores that try to tap into the online world using technologies are at the forefront of offering the optimal shopping experience to customers.

---

9 *'Mobile Commerce Will Be Nearly Half of E-Commerce by 2018', Internet Retailer, SOURCE.*
10 *'US eCommerce Grows, Reaching $414B by 2018, but Physical Stores Will Live On', Forbes, SOURCE.*

The Shopping Process

An understanding of the shopping process is very important. This is why we need to recap what we previously learned in this book. The purchase of every product nowadays is a result of a fairly complex shopping process, which starts off with discovering the product, testing it, pickup or delivery, and in many instances, to returns. The modern day technology-savvy consumers have a crystal clear idea of what they want, including the:

- ✔ Price,
- ✔ Style; and
- ✔ Availability of the product

While having a greater awareness of their needs as well as the options that they have, the consumers of today also focus on enjoying an engaging shopping experience. With so many options available where they can get their desired product from, loyalty often runs short. Brick-and-mortar retailers have to adapt to these changing circumstances and implement the necessary technologies to serve these savvy consumers if they are to gain an edge over their competitors, online and offline alike.

Transformation of the Purchase Cycle

Gone are the days when customers entered a store and were greeted by a salesperson that often ended up selling a product. In those days, the consumers did not have as many options as they have now; nor did they have access to information and deals in just a few clicks.

Consumers choose a channel after considering a wide range of criteria, ranging from brand loyalty to physical convenience to the ultimate desire to be surprised or entertained. Thus, where and how customer value is created and how it is captured, solely depends on the preferences of a consumer. Nonetheless, irrespective of the preferences of the consumers, a study has revealed that brick-and-mortar stores remain the cornerstone of this purchase cycle, which comprises of several steps before an actual purchase takes place.

The buying process starts and involves the following locations:

1. **At Home**

The consumer, when intending to buy a certain product, begins the buying process at home by:

- ▶ Searching online
- ▶ Browsing reviews
- ▶ Creating wish lists
- ▶ Liking companies & products on social media
- ▶ Receiving coupons or offers

2. **To Store**

When on the way to a store, or when roaming around in a mall, consumers use their smartphones to:

- ▶ Locate a store
- ▶ Read product reviews
- ▶ Look at their wish list
- ▶ Receive coupons

3. **In Store**

Statistics indicate that as many as 79 percent of consumers use their smartphones while inside a store for the following purposes:

- ▶ Searching for prices online
- ▶ 'Showrooming'
- ▶ Utilizing loyalty apps
- ▶ Receiving gamification offers & coupons
- ▶ Texting & chatting

4. At Shelf/Rack

When at a particular shelf or rack where their desired product is located, they may use the digital kiosks for more information, sign up for offers, order products to be shipped, and get help.

5. At Purchase

At checkout, consumers can use their smartphones to:
- ▸ Redeem an offer
- ▸ Register their purchase on loyalty app
- ▸ Earn loyalty points

6. Back At Home

After returning home, the vender can follow up the individuals, offer them coupons, ask for product reviews if the consumer purchased a product from them, and carry out targeted advertising.

This, however, would depend on how the vender has implemented technology and whether or not the retailer focuses on omnichannel marketing techniques.

How Consumers Interact with the Digital World

Consumers are now relying heavily on technology and the Internet to make their purchase decisions. As of 2013, around $1.3 million of products have been researched on the Internet before being bought. The question is, how can brick-and-mortar retailers reverse the trend of sales being taken away by online-only retailers?

Showrooming is a practice where merchandise is examined in a physical store by a consumer; however, the purchase is made from an online store, typically at a cheaper rate. This causes the physical retailer to lose a sale.

Reversing the Effects of Showrooming

The iConnect Shopper Intelligence Analytics empowers retailers to take advantage of the trending technology to gain a better understanding of consumers. It aims at helping physical retailers to increase revenue, enhance loyalty, and ensure that their conversion funnel remains full. It also helps retailers by providing them useful information that can be used to plan the amount of staff required in a particular store.

How Brick-and-Mortar Stores Are the Future of Retail

With a rising number of retail choices available, consumers are purchasing more carefully and assertively comparing prices as well as the availability of merchandise from both online and traditional brick-and-mortar retailers. Many consumers tend to carry out research of the deals in-store; however, they often end up making a purchase online from some other retailer, wasting not only the retailers' time but also their resources. Traditional, physical retailers—including those that have a successful online presence—require a new set of techniques in order to draw customers to the retail stores and encourage them to purchase with cut-throat offerings when in the store.

1. Discovery

Discovering new products and offerings is the only stage in the shopping process where consumers prefer to search online for certain categories. Nonetheless, most of the consumers are in favour of in-store discovery for key categories, such as accessories and apparel, beauty and health, and furniture.

In addition to the convenience, such physical retail stores are the preferred choice of consumers looking to find new product ranges.

2. Trial and Test

When the testing or trial of a product is concerned, research has shown that brick-and-mortar stores are the most favourite of consumers. The ease, immediacy, and accuracy of testing the products are some of the reasons that make in-store trials the preferred option.

3. Purchase

Of all retail sales in the US, 90 per cent are carried out at physical stores. Consumers generally prefer these stores due to accessibility and immediacy, which do not seem capable of being replicated by any other forms of purchase. When it comes to categories such as electronics, fine jewellery, sporting goods, and furniture, most consumers prefer stores due to the enhanced customer service that, according to them, is not available online.

4. Delivery/Pickup

Consumers prefer picking up a product from a store over home delivery mainly because of the greater sense of trust and reliability that it offers. Also, there is the added benefit of being able to take a product home right away.

5. Returns

Across all the categories of products, physical stores are indeed the centre for all product returns, including those that have been made online. As a matter of fact, after the testing and trial of products, consumers prefer physical stores for returning products in person.

The Issue of Showrooming

A lot of marketers mistakenly believe that the journey of a customer starts and ends in the same channel. Everyone is a consumer, even the CEO of a business or the director of marketing; we all make purchases and interact with numerous brands and make purchase decisions almost every day.

As we think about this, a question surfaces: how many times do you actually 'touch' brands in your day-to-day life? There are many ways to come in contact with a brand. You can get information about it on social media or through e-mail newsletters, in-store visits, or adverts through any number of different channels. All these types of interactions are actually a part of the entire journey of a customer.

Due to the way that our lives and the technology in our lives have evolved, today's consumers are highly empowered and are piloting their own purchase cycle. No longer are brands able to contain them in a single channel. Customers complete their purchases at a time and place that is suitable and convenient for them, even if it requires them to jump from one channel to another. The brands that try to stop them from moving from one channel to another will annoy, frustrate, and confuse them.

This tendency and ability of consumers to shift between the channels result in some serious issues and challenges for marketers, particularly in terms of attribution; there is no better example than the gap between brick-and-mortar stores and online ones.

Showrooming is yet another term that has been developed based on the trends that stem from fragmentation of a typical customer path towards purchase. *Showrooming* results when a customer heads into an offline store to physically inspect a product or try it out, which is undoubtedly a huge step in making the actual purchase decision, but then makes a purchase online.

This leads to numerous challenges for marketers, including the following:

- A lot of them see showrooming as a huge threat to brick-and-mortar stores, which actually play a major role in the customers' path to purchase. Unfortunately, they do not get the credit in the actual sale.
- Showrooming leads to an increased gap in the journey of the customer. If a customer decides to purchase a product in-store, this decision may be affected when they go online to find the same product at a lower price.

Nevertheless, it all combines to state that the journey of a customer is highly fragmented across numerous devices and between online and offline channels. Retailers need to understand the need to provide an utterly seamless experience, and they must learn to recognise what particular people are actually interested in and then translate this understanding across numerous channels. The ultimate aim is to have that customer check out with them.

Bridging the Gap between Online and Offline Stores

Once marketers and business executives have a clear understanding of the need of having a seamless online and offline experience, it is time to determine which tactics are the most efficient to achieve it.

A breakthrough can be achieved when any brand is able to bring together all its channels to the point that their in-store staff becomes capable of identifying customers in real time, and then using that information, they are able to offer an enhanced shopping experience to the customer.

Using this approach, offline retailers too can mirror the ease and speed of online shopping by using emerging technologies, such as Wi-Fi tracking systems and on-site tablets, which provide the customer the ability to read reviews and browse similar products. This will also enable the store to increase its ability to capture more data for analytical purposes to further optimise its operations.

This will, of course, depend on the level of consumer insight together with the depth of understanding of the target audience. It must also be kept in mind that the consumer of today is very demanding and that customer behaviour is in flux, which means that retailers need to have the latest analytical data regarding customer behaviour if they are to make effective and smart decisions. The building of a single customer view across numerous channels—including mobile, SMS, e-mail, physical, and browsing—is crucial and must become the top priority of all retailers.

Mobile technology is going to play a crucial role in all this as it will provide a link between various locations and the information that has already been gathered about the individual customer. One example of technology that can be used by physical stores to send customers offers that interest them is *geofencing*.

One Brand, Same Enhanced Experience, Multiple Channels

The bridging of the gap between online and offline stores will stand out as a crucial differentiator for retailers. Customers now search for seamless and enjoyable shopping experiences, and adding hurdles or making the shopping process complex will only turn out to be counterproductive to the bottom line of a retailer.

Ultimately, everything boils down to the understanding that the consumer views a **brand as one** instead of viewing every individual channel differently. This should be taken into account when planning to optimise the shopping experience of any consumer.

In today's highly competitive world, where the consumer is very demanding and where consumer behaviour changes constantly, it is crucial to remove any friction from within the shopping experience. This will lead to a seamless and enjoyable shopping experience for the customer, encouraging them to make the purchase while building brand loyalty, which itself plays an important role in helping drive sales.

From Multichannel to Cross-Channel: A Shift in the Approach

Individuals are producing an ever-increasing amount of data from all kinds of devices and through numerous channels. As a result, the way marketers communicate with the consumers is also getting more disparate.

Some e-mail their customers, while some prefer to text. Some display ads without knowing who is actually viewing them, while some have no idea why they are on social media.

What marketers should really be focusing on instead of just creating multiple channels is how they interact with each customer regardless of the channel they use.

Cross-channel is a relatively new term that is increasingly used when discussing the issues of omnichannel marketing. It is crucial to understand what this term means, how it differs from the typical multichannel approach, and what steps should be taken to make this shift successfully.

Cross-channel is the latest trend in marketing strategies, and it has been made possible through various intelligence analytics and complex platforms. It involves marketing to a consumer as a single person across numerous channels. Using this approach, all the channels are linked up and are dependent on one another.

This is what leads to various misconceptions. A lot of businesses may have heard the term *cross-channel marketing,* and many mistakenly claim that they run what they call cross-channel strategy. However, having an active presence on a number of channels is definitely not cross-channel marketing. In fact, it is multichannel marketing.

If your business runs PPC campaigns, a Facebook page, or an e-mail strategy, it does not imply that all these channels are working in conjunction with one another. It may be that similar messages are being sent out on each of the channels as they may be a part of the same marketing campaign; however, unless these channels are linked with one another and communicate together, they are not cross-channel campaigns but, rather, are multichannel in nature.

For instance, when same social media and PPC adverts are put forth for people who have also been sent an e-mail with the same message, this will be regarded as a cross-channel campaign. While the messaging in each of the methods will be a little different, each of the channels will greatly benefit from the other channels' targeted support.

Going Cross-Channel

To be able to properly shift from a multichannel approach to a cross-channel one, your organization will need to concentrate on individuals instead of individual contact points. Stop thinking about customers as a phone number, e-mail address, or a cookie-tracking ID and start thinking of them as people—people with multiple touchpoints. When this way of looking at customers becomes a norm for a company, it becomes a lot simpler to understand how the different channels can support and help one another.

To be able to successfully shift your approach, you need to look into the data of your organization collects. You must join your data to get a cross-channel view of all your consumers so that you are able to identify individuals instead of just points. An individual may have as many as three different e-mail addresses, two social media profiles, and a mobile number. In order to get a cross-channel view of them, you need to combine all the data until you have a single individual instead of a list containing multiple channels. This is referred to as achieving the single-customer view.

With single customer view, you treat people as distinct individuals. This allows organizations to segment individuals and treat each of the segments in the best way possible.

CHAPTER 12: LEVERAGING IT SOLUTIONS

In the area of business analytics, a growing divide is developing between retailers as many of them are taking full advantage of IT solutions and opportunities by transitioning to and implementing technologies.

New tools are emerging to help retailers understand data and use it to their advantage for the purpose of making smart business decisions. As the commerce world continues to go through the digitization process, with the emergence of big data and the constant advancement of technologies for analytical purposes, businesses have significant opportunities to make themselves stand out from the crowd.

A study called *'Analytics: The Widening Divide'*,[11] carried out by MIT Sloan Management Review and IBM Institute for Business Value, states that almost 58 per cent of all businesses now utilise business analytics to gain a competitive advantage over their competitors within their markets or industry. These same businesses are twice more likely to outperform their competition.

The focus of this chapter will be to highlight the importance and need of information management and how businesses and retailers can partner with IT solutions to boost their retail operations and increase their bottom line.

---

11 *'Analytics: The Widening Divide'*, IBM Institute for Business Value, SOURCE.

Building the Foundation for Business Analytics

The retailers that have a strong foundation upon which they gather data and information are more capable of tackling business objectives that are critical to their future and operations. Their strong foundation of data makes it possible for them to capture the data, combine it, and use it from a wide number of sources. They also disseminate the information so that everyone throughout the organization has access to the data, which in turn helps them perform their job well.

An organization's ability to integrate information and data across business and functional silos is of a very crucial importance. This ability makes such businesses 4.9 times more capable of leveraging the power of business analytics for increased bottom line, according to the IBM study.

Information management competency is the use of techniques, methodologies, and technologies that address issues such as data architecture, transformation, extraction, storage, movement, and integration as well as the governance of information and master data management. It involves a wide range of skills and expertise in numerous techniques for developing architecture and managing data for integration, storage, and portability.

Business analytics is crucial in deriving the true value of information management competency.

In today's world, where the amount of data is constantly rising, IT is responsible for ensuring that consistent standards are established to maintain data quality across all the business news as well as functions.

Keep in mind the following questions:
- Is the data extracted from dissimilar data sources, both external and internal, thoroughly and accurately?
- Can the data be used by various business units and functions? Are there specific functions that are working from similar sets of data?
- Is the data gathered compatible with any existing processes? How difficult is it to be able to adjust to any organizational changes?
- Can the data be managed in real time?

This also requires a fairly rigorous approach to governance of data. A structured management approach is designed to track strategic objectives against allocation of any analytical resources. At every level of the company, decision makers can confidently use the information to do their jobs in the most effective manner possible and make smart, informed decisions using analytics to efficiently guide their day-to-day operations as well as future strategies.

Moving Rapidly on Actionable Insights

As we have discussed throughout this book, the needs and wants of customers change rapidly, and a retailer has to quickly respond to such changes by keeping track of customer behaviour through business analytics. While it may be one thing to identify the changes in the behaviour of customers, quickly responding to meet the changes is another. Collaboration is necessary for any retailer to properly respond to the insights received.

Fortunately, business analytics delivers collaboration as well as social networking to propel the exchange of data, activities, and ideas to help with effective decision-making.

People are able to proactively exchange data and knowledge and information in a collaborative environment; they also cooperate more with one another, thereby eliminating any communication barriers within the organization while enhancing the readiness of the organization for anything that comes in the way.

Having access to similar performance data as well as plans diminishes the risk of the information or any actions being lost during transit, and it ensures a smart and informed decision is made, which aligns the actions with the ultimate aim of accomplishing organizational goals. Collaboration effectively closes the ongoing loop from data to insight to action and allows everyone to collectively work together, agree upon things, decide, and act.

How Retailers Can Take Advantage of Emerging Technology

With such extensive use of mobile devices such as smartphones, consumers generate a huge amount of data to search for information, including prices and reviews. In general, retailers mostly see that their sales are gradually decreasing with the advent of online shopping platforms; however, what they do not know is how and why this is happening.

The iConnect Shopper Intelligence Analytics allows retailers to tap into this precious big data and gain business insights and metrics regarding consumer behaviour, staff performance, and foot traffic patterns.

To optimise your store's performance when it comes to serving the consumers, there are three steps that you need to take. The three steps are as follows:
1. **Measure**—Focus on presence and positioning analytics
2. **Connect**—Opt-in marketing and Wi-Fi
3. **Influence**—Real-time, location-based marketing

Measure

The analytic capability of iConnect's Shopper Intelligence solution aims at providing retailers with answers to several most common yet crucial questions.

It provides **traffic flow metrics**, such as the following:
- How much traffic there is outside your store?
- How many consumers enter your store?
- How many consumers stop by your shop's window?
- Are these new consumers or repeat customers?
- How do these numbers compare to last week?

The iConnect Shopper Intelligence also gathers vital data regarding how your consumers move about your store as well as how they are served by your staff (**in-store metrics**). It can help you gather data on the following:
- Which zones attract the most number of shoppers?
- How effective are your methods of drawing shoppers into your store?
- How regularly do customers visit your store and for how long?
- How efficient is your staff in serving customers?
- How effectively is your checkout queue managed?

The great thing about iConnect's Shopper Intelligence Analytics (SIA) proprietary technology is that a customer does not have to make a purchase in order for his or her data to be captured. You can utilise your existing in-store Wi-Fi network to benefit from this analytic tool.

Connect

Retailers can also gain an edge over their competition by implementing location-based marketing (LBM) and opt-in marketing techniques. LBM relies on smartphones and mobile devices to locate a person who is in a close proximity to a certain area. For instance, retailers can attract passersby by sending them relevant promotions that are active to their particular location. These passersby may be roaming around a mall, and location-based marketing can lead them to your store, allowing the SIA to take over from there and gather relevant data.

This technique is highly effective and a causal success factor for brick-and-mortar stores because today's consumers are almost always searching online for the right product or service even when on the go.

Influence

After gathering data using iConnect's Shopper Intelligence Analytics tool, retailers can take steps to target the audience and consumers more effectively. This can be achieved by offering consumers coupons, deals, and loyalty cards and by formulating effectual marketing campaigns to drive more store traffic.

These three steps are crucial for physical retailers in order to increase revenue and draw in more customers while increasing conversion rates. However, all this cannot be achieved without the help of today's latest technologies.

IT and Business: Delivering Constant Improvements

Business analytics assists in driving retail sales to a position where the organization is able to outperform its competitors easily without too much hassle. The following step-by-step approach can help your organization to effectively work towards its vision:

- ✓ Start anywhere, growing the investment in analytical tools as required by your company.
- ✓ Take insight to action to make sure that strategic decisions are taken at the point of impact.
- ✓ Satisfy the individual, team, and the company-wide needs by having the right type of analytics for your company.
- ✓ Deliver value at each and every step through business analytics.
- ✓ Balance control and freedom through analytics to empower the business user and make sure you respect IT standards.

If this seems to be overwhelming, stop for a while and relax. You don't have to get everything up and running by yourself. To effectively drive value from analytics, you need to establish partnership between numerous sections within your organization and increase collaboration, such as between sales to finances to marketing to the IT department.

IT can assist you by recommending the right tools, by layering the business analytics tools, and by giving other departments access to the technologies.

Business analytics can offer actionable insights together with performance management capabilities to each and every department of your organization, ranging from marketing to operations to finance. It can tailor the requirements of every decision maker in the organization, from the board level down to the shop floor. These abilities significantly reduce the costs while improving business performance and by strengthening the overall retail operations.

CONCLUSION

As the retail environment continues to change because of the constant flux in customer behaviour, all retailers need to adapt to technologies that can assist them in providing an enhanced shopping experience to their consumer base. The need to implement technologies, such as Wi-Fi tracking solutions and the like, has been bolstered by the rapid expansion of e-commerce.

Today, e-commerce channels are capable of providing convenience to customers, allowing them to purchase whatever they desire right from the comfort of their homes. The Internet and mobile devices enable them to conveniently search and compare prices.

Nonetheless, even though e-commerce has been expanding at a fast pace, it has not and cannot provide the human element in the shopping experience. People love to be able to check out a product before they actually buy it, and this can only be accomplished at a brick-and-mortar store. This is exactly what has led to the concept of showrooming, a scenario where customers check out the product at a particular store and then purchase it online from a different company.

This shift in consumer patterns has made it crucial for offline retailers to turn towards technology and use it to provide a comprehensive shopping experience—one that provides their consumers multiple channels to search from and purchase products while being able to enjoy the human element by visiting a physical store.

The modern consumer is far more knowledgeable, has many options, and is now at the helm of the retail industry as they steer through countless technological advances and developments made available for them.

While it is true that e-commerce has had a significant impact on the sales and bottom line of physical stores, it is good to see that many smart offline retailers are beginning to understand what it takes to attract customers despite the changes in the industry.

Online shopping websites and portals have always had an edge over retail stores with regards to the options of analytical tools available to them. Online stores have leveraged techniques to learn about the habits of their customers and have used it to their advantage by offering as well as suggesting products and services based on the behaviour of the consumers. They have benefited from this for quite some time now.

However, the technology and technique to help brick-and-mortar stores to better understand the behaviour of their customers are emerging at a pace never expected before, and many retailers have already implemented such tools, with more of them planning to do so in the near future.

These tools enable brick-and-mortar stores to gather crucial analytics to understand shopping trends and consumer behaviour while using the gathered data to make smart business decisions. By leveraging IT solutions, offline retailers have the ability to regain their past glory and offer a mesh of offline and online services for a better consumer experience.

ABOUT AMITESH SINHA

Amitesh Sinha is a contemporary technology consultant based in North America with over twenty years of hands-on experience in developing and deploying innovative solutions for retail, specifically providing services to furniture retailers, which include many Ashley HomeStores and a few others. Mr. Sinha's credentials have made him significantly distinguished among home-furnishing technology providers due to his extending contribution in the development and successful deployment of retail furniture software, analytics, and reengineering of software, with extended features and support.

A progressive, decisive, innovative individual highly valued for expertise, interpreting corporate vision and strategy, translating objectives into actionable plans, and providing decisive leadership to multi-functional and cross-cultural teams, Mr. Sinha has the professional synergies that make him a significant choice for commercial and government agencies, where he has been successful in delivering cutting-edge solutions and services according to the company demands and contemporary business requirements. He is in the list of topmost furniture consultants, retail consultants, and retail home-furnishing specialists, facilitating Ashley HomeStores and providing a centralised, unified, and easily replicated database system to perform their query operations on a single click.

Sinha earned his MBA from JBIMS, Mumbai, India, and started his professional career from Stock Holding Corporation of India Limited and served there for seven years. In 2000, he moved to the USA and established the iConnect group, a professional consultancy business with a focus on technology management and delivering services.

The iConnect group currently works with top-notch companies to steer short-term and long-term technology strategies and provide flexible solutions by anticipating their needs and requirements.

INDEX

A

AA (Advanced Analytics) 29, 44, 46-7, 62, 68
access points (AP) 35
accuracy 36, 39, 44, 62, 67, 87
advanced analytics (AA) 46
analytical applications 28-9
analytical data 2-3, 25, 27, 29, 33-4, 63, 70, 88
Analytical Decision Management (ADM) 47
analytical tools 5, 26, 28-30, 94-5
analytics 2-3, 5, 12, 16, 18, 25-31, 34-5, 37, 39, 43-6, 48-51, 54, 56-72, 86, 91-5
AP (access points) 35, 37-8, 40

B

behaviour 5, 16, 18, 26-30, 34-7, 45, 53-4, 57, 59-60, 63, 68, 88, 92-3, 95
blogs 56-7, 69, 74
brand loyalty 19, 26, 45-6, 66-70, 85, 88
brands 26, 55, 67-70, 73, 75-6, 83-4, 87
brick-and-mortar retailers 13, 19, 22, 35, 76, 85-6
business analytics 3, 16, 18, 43-6, 49-51, 54, 56-63, 66-72, 91-2, 94
business intelligence (BI) 46
business owners 2, 5, 12-13

C

clustering 31
competition 5, 9-10, 13, 16, 18, 53, 58-9, 70, 84, 91, 93
complaints 57, 76
consumer base 28, 95
consumer behaviour 5, 30, 36, 53-4, 59, 88, 93, 95
consumer data 50-1, 54
consumer demographics 63
consumer profiles 34
consumer satisfaction 70
consumers 2, 5, 7-10, 12-13, 15-23, 25-6, 33-7, 40, 43-5, 53-60, 63, 67-70, 75-6, 83-7, 93-5
content analytics 56-7
context 54-5, 76
control 2, 12, 17, 29, 34, 36, 62-3, 82, 94
convenience 8-9, 12, 16, 19, 63, 67-8, 83-5, 87, 95
corporate strategy 50-1, 71
cross-channel campaigns 89
customer data 43, 54, 58

customer experience 13, 37, 66-7, 69, 82
customer loyalty 18, 26-8, 44, 50-1, 54, 63-5, 70-1
customer service 2, 27, 55, 64, 66, 68, 70, 76, 87

D

data classification process 39
decision makers 5, 18, 49-50, 68, 71, 92
decision-making 17, 45-8, 50, 55-6, 59, 62, 80, 92
demands 16, 25, 27, 44-5, 47-8, 56, 59, 62, 66-7, 69, 75, 97
demographic insights 60
devices 5, 13, 16-17, 30, 34-9, 63-5, 69, 88-9, 93, 95
digital era 67
digital signage 63-5
digital world 86

E

e-commerce 2-3, 5, 8-10, 21-3, 25, 51, 76, 83-4, 95
e-commerce platforms 9-10
e-commerce sales 23, 84
enterprise data warehouse (EDW) 29
entrepreneurs 7-8

F

Facebook 44, 69, 73-5, 89
feedback 39, 56-7, 67, 74-5, 77
foot traffic 12, 41, 63, 93
footprints 15
forecasting 30-1, 67, 71-2, 80
forecasts 30-1, 47, 50-1, 65-6, 72
Forrester Research 13, 23
fraud 30, 58
frequency 37, 40, 64

I

IBM Institute for Business Value 16, 91
iConnect 35, 37-41, 63-4, 86, 93-4, 97
identifier 41
integration 29, 60, 64-7, 71, 92
Internet 5, 8-10, 12-13, 16-17, 22, 34-6, 55-6, 63, 74, 76, 84, 86, 95
inventory 9, 12-13, 17, 26, 30, 50, 60-3, 66, 79
investments 19, 26, 35, 37, 62, 70

K

key performance indicators (KPIs) 50, 80

L

line busting 63-4
localization 31
location-based marketing (LBM) 93
locations 19, 35, 41, 45, 85, 88
logs 34, 43, 82
loyalty 16, 18-20, 26-30, 44-6, 50-1, 54, 57-8, 60, 63-71, 75, 77, 85-6, 88, 94

M

MAC address 34, 40-1
market basket analysis 58
marketing 11, 16, 18, 20, 26-7, 29-31, 35, 50, 53-5, 57-8, 60, 66-72, 86-7, 89, 93-4
marketing campaigns 35, 58, 70, 94
marketing mix modelling 31
marketing strategies 53, 69, 89
markets 10, 17, 22-3, 26, 48, 58, 73, 91
mobile commerce 69, 83-4
mobile devices 16-17, 30, 35-7, 65, 69, 93, 95
mobile phones 13
multichannel approach 89

N

National Retail Federation (NRF) 7, 11
network 21, 37, 39-40, 63-5, 93
nonstore retailing 10

O

offline retailers 88, 95
offline sales channels 75
omnichannel 13, 17, 19-20, 22, 44, 58, 64-8, 86, 89
online retailers 2, 13, 25, 35, 84
online services 63, 95
online shopping websites 5, 27, 95
operational decisions 47, 49
operations 9-10, 22, 28, 37, 43, 46-7, 50, 63-4, 66, 70-2, 79, 81, 84, 91-2, 94
out of stock 26, 62, 80
oversampling 39-40

P

performance management (PM) 47
physical retailers 86, 94
point of sales (POS) 84
purchase cycle 19, 85, 87

R

real-time information 49
risk management 47-8

S

self-service 63
Shopper Intelligence Analytics (SIA) 93
shopping process 19, 85-6, 88
showrooming 20, 22, 25-6, 85-8, 95
shrink 80
social media 16-17, 19, 26, 53, 56, 63-4, 67, 69-70, 73-7, 85, 87, 89
social responsibility 11
store retailing 8
supply chain 28, 37, 43, 47, 55, 60, 62, 65-6

T

time stamp 38, 40
tools 5, 12, 26-31, 34-5, 45, 49, 51, 59, 62-4, 68-70, 72, 74, 77, 79-81, 94-5
top-down plans 61
trends 5, 13, 26, 28-9, 35, 37, 44, 54-5, 57, 59-60, 62-3, 68, 75, 77, 87
trust 5, 12, 30, 60, 70, 87
Twitter 44, 69, 73-4

U

undersampling 39
unstructured data 55-6

V

value chain 66-7, 73
visibility 46-7, 49, 66, 72

W

websites 2, 5, 13, 27, 29, 34, 40, 57, 74, 76-7, 95
Wi-Fi Analytics 29
Wi-Fi network 37, 64-5, 93
Wi-Fi Shopper Intelligence Analytics 29, 68
Wi-Fi signals 37-8
Wi-Fi tracking 2-3, 27, 34-5, 44, 64, 88, 95

Z

zones 65, 93

Copyedited and indexed by Gienel Aberca
Reviewed by Jeffrey James Torres

Printed in the United States
By Bookmasters